MAX LUCADO

Life Lessons *from*

1 SAMUEL

Israel Becomes a Kingdom

Harper*Christian*
Resources

CONTENTS

HOW TO STUDY THE BIBLE

The Bible is a peculiar book. Words crafted in another language. Deeds done in a distant era. Events recorded in a far-off land. Counsel offered to a foreign people. It is a peculiar book.

It's surprising that anyone reads it. It's too old. Some of its writings date back 5,000 years. It's too bizarre. The book speaks of incredible floods, fires, earthquakes, and people with supernatural abilities. It's too radical. The Bible calls for undying devotion to a carpenter who called himself God's Son.

Logic says this book shouldn't survive. Too old, too bizarre, too radical.

The Bible has been banned, burned, scoffed, and ridiculed. Scholars have mocked it as foolish. Kings have branded it as illegal. A thousand times over the grave has been dug and the dirge has begun, but somehow the Bible never stays in the grave. Not only has it survived, but it has also thrived. It is the single most popular book in all of history. It has been the bestselling book in the world for years!

There is no way on earth to explain it. Which perhaps is the only explanation. For the Bible's durability is not found on *earth* but in *heaven*. The millions who have tested its claims and claimed its promises know there is but one answer: the Bible is God's book and God's voice.

As you read it, you would be wise to give some thought to two questions: *What is the purpose of the Bible?* and *How do I study the Bible?* Time spent reflecting on these two issues will greatly enhance your Bible study.

What is the purpose of the Bible?

Let the Bible itself answer that question: *"From infancy you have known the Holy Scriptures, which are able to make you wise for salvation through faith in Christ Jesus"* (2 Timothy 3:15).

The purpose of the Bible? Salvation. God's highest passion is to get his children home. His book, the Bible, describes his plan of salvation. The purpose of the Bible is to proclaim God's plan and passion to save his children.

This is the reason why this book has endured through the centuries. It dares to tackle the toughest questions about life: *Where do I go after I die? Is there a God? What do I do with my fears?* The Bible is the treasure map that leads to God's highest treasure—eternal life.

But how do you study the Bible? Countless copies of Scripture sit unread on bookshelves and nightstands simply because people don't know how to read it. What can you do to make the Bible real in your life?

The clearest answer is found in the words of Jesus: *"Ask and it will be given to you; seek and you will find; knock and the door will be opened to you"* (Matthew 7:7).

The first step in understanding the Bible is asking God to help you. You should read it prayerfully. If anyone understands God's Word, it is because of God and not the reader.

"The Advocate, the Holy Spirit, whom the Father will send in my name, will teach you all things and will remind you of everything I have said to you" (John 14:26).

Before reading the Bible, pray and invite God to speak to you. Don't go to Scripture looking for your idea, but go searching for his.

Not only should you read the Bible prayerfully, but you should also read it carefully. *"Seek and you will find"* is the pledge. The Bible is not a newspaper to be skimmed but rather a mine to be quarried. *"If you look for it as for silver and search for it as for hidden treasure, then you will understand the fear of the LORD and find the knowledge of God"* (Proverbs 2:4–5).

Any worthy find requires effort. The Bible is no exception. To understand the Bible, you don't have to be brilliant, but you must be willing to roll up your sleeves and search.

"Do your best to present yourself to God as one approved, a worker who does not need to be ashamed and who correctly handles the word of truth" (2 Timothy 2:15).

Here's a practical point. Study the Bible a bit at a time. Hunger is not satisfied by eating twenty-one meals in one sitting once a week. The body needs a steady diet to remain strong. So does the soul. When God sent food to his people in the wilderness, he didn't provide loaves already made. Instead, he sent them manna in the shape of *"thin flakes like frost on the ground"* (Exodus 16:14).

God gave manna in limited portions.

God sends spiritual food the same way. He opens the heavens with just enough nutrients for today's hunger. He provides *"a rule for this, a rule for that; a little here, a little there"* (Isaiah 28:10).

Don't be discouraged if your reading reaps a small harvest. Some days a lesser portion is all that is needed. What is important is to search every day for that day's message. A steady diet of God's Word over a lifetime builds a healthy soul and mind.

It's much like the little girl who returned from her first day at school feeling a bit dejected. Her mom asked, "Did you learn anything?"

"Apparently not enough," the girl responded. "I have to go back tomorrow, and the next day, and the next … "

Such is the case with learning. And such is the case with Bible study. Understanding comes little by little over a lifetime.

There is a third step in understanding the Bible. After the asking and seeking comes the knocking. After you ask and search, *"knock and the door will be opened to you"* (Matthew 7:7).

To knock is to stand at God's door. To make yourself available. To climb the steps, cross the porch, stand at the doorway, and volunteer. Knocking goes beyond the realm of thinking and into the realm of acting.

To knock is to ask, *What can I do? How can I obey? Where can I go?*

It's one thing to know what to do. It's another to do it. But for those who do it—those who choose to obey—a special reward awaits them.

"Whoever looks intently into the perfect law that gives freedom, and continues in it—not forgetting what they have heard, but doing it—they will be blessed in what they do" (James 1:25).

What a promise. Blessings come to those who do what they read in God's Word! It's the same with medicine. If you only read the label but ignore the pills, it won't help. It's the same with food. If you only read the recipe but never cook, you won't be fed. And it's the same with the Bible. If you only read the words but never obey, you'll never know the joy God has promised.

Ask. Search. Knock. Simple, isn't it? So why don't you give it a try? If you do, you'll see why the Bible is the most remarkable book in history.

INTRODUCTION TO

The Book of 1 Samuel

It's the end of the race that matters.

Trophies aren't given for great starts. Medals aren't awarded for entering the race. A good start is crucial, but in the end, the end is all that matters.

First Samuel is a book of good starts but bad finishes.

It seems that every key character put his best foot forward and ended up in last place. Take Eli for example.

A sterling religious leader. A man with a heart for God. Perceptive and strong, the last of the great priests. But look at the end of his life. The ark of the covenant has been captured. Two of his rebellious sons are killed. When he hears of their deaths, he falls over and breaks his neck. Samuel is another case. Dedicated to God's service by Hannah, his mother, he anointed Israel's first kings. But he didn't learn from Eli's mistakes. Just like his mentor, he failed to train his family and his sons turned away from God.

But the most dramatic example is Saul, Israel's first king. He seemed to be the perfect man—handsome and meek, brave and victorious in battle. But success led to disobedience, and he slid from prominence to paranoia to suicide.

Why are these stories in the Bible? To remind us that we, too, are in a race. And that race isn't over. How we started isn't nearly as important as how we finish.

AUTHOR AND DATE

The author of 1 and 2 Samuel (originally one book) is unknown, though Jewish tradition held that it was written by Samuel himself along with the prophets Nathan and Gad (based on 1 Chronicles 29:29). Given that Samuel's death is recorded in 1 Samuel 25:1, he could only be the author of the first twenty-four chapters, with Nathan and Gad writing the rest. A note in 1 Samuel 27:6 describing how the city of Ziklag was given "to the kings of Judah" seems to indicate that the work was penned after the rule of Solomon when the kingdom was divided between Israel and Judah in 931 BC. If this is the case—and the note was not added at a later time—it would rule out the possibility of Samuel, Nathan, or Gad being the authors, as they all operated either before or during the rule of David. There is no clear indication as to how late the writing could be, but most likely it was penned before the exile, thus c. 931–722 BC.

SITUATION

The events in 1 Samuel begin at the close of a time in Israel's history known as the period of the judges. At the time, Israel was at a low point spiritually. Eli, who served as priest and judge in Shiloh, had two sons who were also priests. These two men were corrupt, and Eli was ineffective in getting them to change their ways. It was only after Samuel became a prophet and judge over Israel that the situation began to change. Most of the action that follows in 1 Samuel takes place in and around the central highlands of Israel, where the major towns were located: Shiloh (home of Eli and the tabernacle), Ramah (hometown of Samuel), Gibeah (headquarters of Saul), and Bethlehem (the birthplace of David). At the time, the greatest threats to the Israelites were from the Ammonites to the east and the Philistines to the west. The Philistines were especially problematic in that they controlled the use of iron, which gave them a military and economic advantage over the Israelites. It was primarily due to this threat, and the fact that Samuel's sons also did not follow God's way, that the people began to demand a king. This led to the transition of Israel being ruled by judges to being ruled by kings.

KEY THEMES

- Samuel's birth was a product of his mother's faith and prayer.
- Israel rejected God as their divine king and demanded a human king.
- Saul lost his power and even his sanity when he refused to obey God.
- God raised up David and gave him victory because of his faith.

KEY VERSE

"Has the LORD *as great delight in burnt offerings and sacrifices, as in obeying the voice of the* LORD*? Behold, to obey is better than sacrifice, and to heed than the fat of rams"* (1 Samuel 15:22 NKJV).

CONTENTS

I. Samuel's Rise to Power as Judge (1:1–7:17)
II. Saul's Rise to Power as King (8:1–16:23)
III. David's Rise to Power as King (17:1–31:13)

HEARING GOD'S VOICE

Samuel said, "Speak, for your servant is listening."
1 SAMUEL 3:10

REFLECTION

What are some of the biggest questions you have when it comes to hearing God's voice?

_____

_____

_____

_____

_____

_____

_____

_____

_____

_____

SITUATION

The story of Israel becoming a kingdom begins in the final years of Eli, a priest who also served as a "judge" over the people. These judges were not necessarily officials who decided legal matters but leaders God raised up over a period of some two hundred years to guide his people and help them defeat their enemies. Eli served at the tabernacle in Shiloh, and one day he saw a woman praying there whom he thought was drunk. As it turns out, this woman, named Hannah, was barren (a sign of disgrace at the time) and was pleading with the Lord to give her a son. Hannah vowed that if God did this, she would dedicate him to the Lord's service. God did give Hannah a son, whom she named Samuel, and when the boy was two to three years old, she fulfilled her vow by bringing him to Eli to serve at the tabernacle. Samuel grew "in stature and in favor with the Lord and with people" (1 Samuel 2:26). However, Eli's two sons, who also served as priests, were only growing in wickedness.

OBSERVATION

Read 1 Samuel 3:1–21 from the New International
Version or the New King James Version.

NEW INTERNATIONAL VERSION

¹ The boy Samuel ministered before the LORD under Eli. In those days the word of the LORD was rare; there were not many visions.

² One night Eli, whose eyes were becoming so weak that he could barely see, was lying down in his usual place. ³ The lamp of God had not yet gone out, and Samuel was lying down in the house of the LORD, where the ark of God was. ⁴ Then the LORD called Samuel.

Samuel answered, "Here I am." ⁵ And he ran to Eli and said, "Here I am; you called me."

But Eli said, "I did not call; go back and lie down." So he went and lay down.

⁶ Again the LORD called, "Samuel!" And Samuel got up and went to Eli and said, "Here I am; you called me."

"My son," Eli said, "I did not call; go back and lie down."

⁷ Now Samuel did not yet know the LORD: The word of the LORD had not yet been revealed to him.

⁸ A third time the LORD called, "Samuel!" And Samuel got up and went to Eli and said, "Here I am; you called me."

Then Eli realized that the LORD was calling the boy. ⁹ So Eli told Samuel, "Go and lie down, and if he calls you, say, 'Speak, LORD, for your servant is listening.'" So Samuel went and lay down in his place.

¹⁰ The LORD came and stood there, calling as at the other times, "Samuel! Samuel!"

Then Samuel said, "Speak, for your servant is listening."

¹¹ And the LORD said to Samuel: "See, I am about to do something in Israel that will make the ears of everyone who hears about it tingle. ¹² At that time I will carry out against Eli everything I spoke against his family—from beginning to end. ¹³ For I told him that I would

judge his family forever because of the sin he knew about; his sons blasphemed God, and he failed to restrain them. [14] Therefore I swore to the house of Eli, 'The guilt of Eli's house will never be atoned for by sacrifice or offering.'"

[15] Samuel lay down until morning and then opened the doors of the house of the Lord. He was afraid to tell Eli the vision, [16] but Eli called him and said, "Samuel, my son."

Samuel answered, "Here I am."

[17] "What was it he said to you?" Eli asked. "Do not hide it from me. May God deal with you, be it ever so severely, if you hide from me anything he told you." [18] So Samuel told him everything, hiding nothing from him. Then Eli said, "He is the Lord; let him do what is good in his eyes."

[19] The Lord was with Samuel as he grew up, and he let none of Samuel's words fall to the ground. [20] And all Israel from Dan to Beersheba recognized that Samuel was attested as a prophet of the Lord. [21] The Lord continued to appear at Shiloh, and there he revealed himself to Samuel through his word.

NEW KING JAMES VERSION

[1] Now the boy Samuel ministered to the Lord before Eli. And the word of the Lord was rare in those days; there was no widespread revelation. [2] And it came to pass at that time, while Eli was lying down in his place, and when his eyes had begun to grow so dim that he could not see, [3] and before the lamp of God went out in the tabernacle of the Lord where the ark of God was, and while Samuel was lying down, [4] that the Lord called Samuel. And he answered, "Here I am!" [5] So he ran to Eli and said, "Here I am, for you called me."

And he said, "I did not call; lie down again." And he went and lay down.

[6] Then the Lord called yet again, "Samuel!"

So Samuel arose and went to Eli, and said, "Here I am, for you called me." He answered, "I did not call, my son; lie down again." [7] (Now Samuel did not yet know the LORD, nor was the word of the LORD yet revealed to him.)

⁸ And the LORD called Samuel again the third time. So he arose and went to Eli, and said, "Here I am, for you did call me."

Then Eli perceived that the LORD had called the boy. ⁹ Therefore Eli said to Samuel, "Go, lie down; and it shall be, if He calls you, that you must say, 'Speak, LORD, for Your servant hears.'" So Samuel went and lay down in his place.

¹⁰ Now the LORD came and stood and called as at other times, "Samuel! Samuel!"

And Samuel answered, "Speak, for Your servant hears."

¹¹ Then the LORD said to Samuel: "Behold, I will do something in Israel at which both ears of everyone who hears it will tingle. ¹² In that day I will perform against Eli all that I have spoken concerning his house, from beginning to end. ¹³ For I have told him that I will judge his house forever for the iniquity which he knows, because his sons made themselves vile, and he did not restrain them. ¹⁴ And therefore I have sworn to the house of Eli that the iniquity of Eli's house shall not be atoned for by sacrifice or offering forever."

¹⁵ So Samuel lay down until morning, and opened the doors of the house of the LORD. And Samuel was afraid to tell Eli the vision. ¹⁶ Then Eli called Samuel and said, "Samuel, my son!"

He answered, "Here I am."

¹⁷ And he said, "What is the word that the LORD spoke to you? Please do not hide it from me. God do so to you, and more also, if you hide anything from me of all the things that He said to you." ¹⁸ Then Samuel told him everything, and hid nothing from him. And he said, "It is the LORD. Let Him do what seems good to Him."

¹⁹ So Samuel grew, and the LORD was with him and let none of his words fall to the ground. ²⁰ And all Israel from Dan to Beersheba knew that Samuel had been established as a prophet of the LORD. ²¹ Then the LORD appeared again in Shiloh. For the LORD revealed Himself to Samuel in Shiloh by the word of the LORD.

EXPLORATION

1. At the time that God called Samuel, "the word of the LORD was rare" in Israel (verse 1). In fact, even though Samuel had lived in the tabernacle his entire life, he evidently did not know God. What does this say about the spiritual leadership at the time?

_____

_____

_____

2. Why do you think God chose to simply call out Samuel's name instead of using more direct (or more forceful) means of getting his attention?

_____

_____

_____

3. The Lord called Samuel's name not once . . . not twice . . . but _three times. What do you think God was trying to teach Samuel by repeatedly calling to him in this manner?_

_____

_____

_____

4. Eli finally realized it was God was calling Samuel. What did he instruct the boy to say the next time the Lord spoke? Why was it important for Samuel to respond this way?

_____

_____

_____

5. God had previously warned Eli that his sons would face judgment for the sins they were committing (see 1 Samuel 2:27–3.6)—but they did not repent. What did God reiterate to Samuel would happen to them? What fault did God find with Eli in this matter?

6. This was the first prophecy that Samuel received from God—but not the last. What did the people throughout Israel soon come to recognize about Samuel?

INSPIRATION

"The LORD came and stood there, calling as at the other times, 'Samuel! Samuel!' Then Samuel said, 'Speak, for your servant is listening'" (1 Samuel 3:10). Prayer, in its purest form, is simply communication with God. We speak. He listens. He speaks. We listen. God changes his people through such moments.

But if we're honest, prayer is odd. It's peculiar. Speaking into space and lifting words into the sky. We can't even get the cable company to answer us, yet God will? The doctor is too busy, but God isn't? We have our doubts about prayer.

And we have our checkered history with prayer: unmet expectations, unanswered requests. We can barely genuflect for the scar tissue on our knees. God, to some, is the ultimate heartbreaker. Why keep tossing the coins of our longings into a silent pool? He jilted me once . . . but not twice. Oh, the peculiar puzzle of prayer.

We aren't the first to struggle. The sign-up sheet for Prayer 101 contains some familiar names: the apostles John, James, Andrew, and Peter. When one of Jesus' disciples requested, "Lord, teach us to pray" (Luke 11:1), none of the others objected. No one walked away saying, "Hey, I have prayer figured out." The first followers of Jesus needed prayer guidance.

In fact, the only tutorial they ever requested was on prayer. They could have asked for instructions on many topics: bread multiplying, speech making, storm stilling. Jesus raised people from the dead. But a "How to Vacate the Cemetery" seminar? His followers never called for one. But they did want him to do this: "Lord, teach us to pray."

This much is sure: God will teach you to pray. He will be patient with you, just as he was with Samuel—calling out his name three times. Don't think for a minute that God is glaring at you from a distance with crossed arms and a scowl, waiting for you to get your prayer life together. Just the opposite. "Here I am! I stand at the door and knock. If you hear my voice and open the door, I will come in and eat with you, and you will eat with me" (Revelation 3:20 NCV).

Jesus waits on the porch. He stands on the threshold. He taps . . . and calls. He waits for you to open the door. To pray is to open it. Prayer is the hand of faith on the door handle of your heart. The willing pull. The happy welcome to Jesus: "Come in, O King. Come in. The kitchen is messy, but come in." (From *Before Amen* by Max Lucado.)

REACTION

7. What are some of the doubts that you have had about prayer? What difficulties, if any, do you have in believing that God hears you when you pray and will answer you?

8. What about your checkered history with prayer? What are some of your unmet expectations or unanswered requests when it comes to prayer?

9. How does it encourage you to know that even the disciples needed guidance on prayer?

10. God was patient in helping Samuel learn how to recognize his voice. How has God been patient with you in the past? How have you learned to recognize his voice?

11. Jesus stands on the threshold of your heart. He taps . . . and calls . . . and waits for you to open the door. What, if anything, is preventing you from accepting his invitation?

12. Paul states that the Holy Spirit will help you in your weakness and intercede for you (see Romans 8:26). What work do you need the Holy Spirit to do in your life today?

_____

_____

_____

_____

_____

_____

_____

LIFE LESSONS

Samuel's only qualification for hearing from the Lord appears to be his willingness to hear. Samuel was only a boy when God spoke to him. In that time, "the word of the LORD was rare" (1 Samuel 3:1), so at first he didn't even recognize that it was *God* doing the talking . . . he thought it was Eli. Even then, what we find in Samuel's story is a young boy leaping out of bed without complaint and rushing to his master's side—and then obeying Eli's direction to invite the Lord to speak. This is the attitude that God wants all his servants to have. Jesus said, "Whoever belongs to God hears what God says" (John 8:47). Those who belong to God desire to hear from God and then do what he says—regardless of how difficult it may be.

DEVOTION

Heavenly Father, we are so thankful that you are willing to speak with us today. Please teach us how to hear your voice—and help us to be open so we will not miss your call. We ask that you continue to instruct us on how to pray so that we will stay in close fellowship with you.

JOURNALING

Samuel said to the Lord, "Speak, for your servant is listening" (1 Samuel 3:10). What do you think would change in your life if you consistently prayed this same prayer?

FOR FURTHER READING

To complete the book of 1 Samuel during this twelve-part study, read 1 Samuel 1:1–3:21. For more Bible passages about hearing God's voice, read Psalm 32:8–9; Isaiah 30:21; Jeremiah 33:3; John 8:47; 10:27; 14:26; Romans 10:17; Revelation 3:20.

A BAD TURN OF EVENTS

"Let us bring the ark of the LORD's covenant from Shiloh, so that he may go with us and save us from the hand of our enemies."
1 SAMUEL 4:3

REFLECTION

What are some of the ways that people try to "bargain" with God to get him to do what they want? What is the danger in thinking a person could ever manipulate God?

_____

_____

_____

_____

_____

_____

_____

_____

_____

_____

_____

_____

SITUATION

God had spoken to Samuel and delivered the news that Eli's two sons would face divine judgment. The years passed, and Samuel became known throughout Israel "as a prophet of the LORD" (1 Samuel 3:20). Meanwhile, Eli's sons continued to act as priests. At the time, the ark of the covenant was housed in the tabernacle at Shiloh, and it seems the Israelites had come to recognize it as a form of "good luck" charm that would ensure their success in battle. So, when the Israelites suffered a defeat by the Philistines, the elders determined to retrieve the ark and take it with the soldiers into the next battle. This decision would result in disaster for the people of Israel—and bring about God's promised judgment against Eli and his sons.

OBSERVATION

*Read 1 Samuel 4:1–18 from the New International
Version or the New King James Version.*

NEW INTERNATIONAL VERSION

[1] Now the Israelites went out to fight against the Philistines. The Israelites camped at Ebenezer, and the Philistines at Aphek. [2] The Philistines deployed their forces to meet Israel, and as the battle spread, Israel was defeated by the Philistines, who killed about four thousand of them on the battlefield. [3] When the soldiers returned to camp, the elders of Israel asked, "Why did the LORD bring defeat on us today before the Philistines? Let us bring the ark of the LORD's covenant from Shiloh, so that he may go with us and save us from the hand of our enemies."

[4] So the people sent men to Shiloh, and they brought back the ark of the covenant of the LORD Almighty, who is enthroned between the cherubim. And Eli's two sons, Hophni and Phinehas, were there with the ark of the covenant of God.

[5] When the ark of the LORD's covenant came into the camp, all Israel raised such a great shout that the ground shook. [6] Hearing the uproar, the Philistines asked, "What's all this shouting in the Hebrew camp?"

When they learned that the ark of the LORD had come into the camp, [7] the Philistines were afraid. "A god has come into the camp," they said. "Oh no! Nothing like this has happened before. [8] We're doomed! Who will deliver us from the hand of these mighty gods? They are the gods who struck the Egyptians with all kinds of plagues in the wilderness. [9] Be strong, Philistines! Be men, or you will be subject to the Hebrews, as they have been to you. Be men, and fight!"

[10] So the Philistines fought, and the Israelites were defeated and every man fled to his tent. The slaughter was very great; Israel lost thirty thousand foot soldiers. [11] The ark of God was captured, and Eli's two sons, Hophni and Phinehas, died.

[12] That same day a Benjamite ran from the battle line and went to Shiloh with his clothes torn and dust on his head. [13] When he arrived,

there was Eli sitting on his chair by the side of the road, watching, because his heart feared for the ark of God. When the man entered the town and told what had happened, the whole town sent up a cry.

¹⁴ Eli heard the outcry and asked, "What is the meaning of this uproar?"

The man hurried over to Eli, ¹⁵ who was ninety-eight years old and whose eyes had failed so that he could not see. ¹⁶ He told Eli, "I have just come from the battle line; I fled from it this very day."

Eli asked, "What happened, my son?"

¹⁷ The man who brought the news replied, "Israel fled before the Philistines, and the army has suffered heavy losses. Also your two sons, Hophni and Phinehas, are dead, and the ark of God has been captured."

¹⁸ When he mentioned the ark of God, Eli fell backward off his chair by the side of the gate. His neck was broken and he died, for he was an old man, and he was heavy. He had led Israel forty years.

NEW KING JAMES VERSION

¹ And the word of Samuel came to all Israel. Now Israel went out to battle against the Philistines, and encamped beside Ebenezer; and the Philistines encamped in Aphek. ² Then the Philistines put themselves in battle array against Israel. And when they joined battle, Israel was defeated by the Philistines, who killed about four thousand men of the army in the field. ³ And when the people had come into the camp, the elders of Israel said, "Why has the LORD defeated us today before the Philistines? Let us bring the ark of the covenant of the LORD from Shiloh to us, that when it comes among us it may save us from the hand of our enemies." ⁴ So the people sent to Shiloh, that they might bring from there the ark of the covenant of the LORD of hosts, who dwells between the cherubim. And the two sons of Eli, Hophni and Phinehas, were there with the ark of the covenant of God.

⁵ And when the ark of the covenant of the LORD came into the camp, all Israel shouted so loudly that the earth shook. ⁶ Now when

the Philistines heard the noise of the shout, they said, "What does the sound of this great shout in the camp of the Hebrews mean?" Then they understood that the ark of the LORD had come into the camp. [7] So the Philistines were afraid, for they said, "God has come into the camp!" And they said, "Woe to us! For such a thing has never happened before. [8] Woe to us! Who will deliver us from the hand of these mighty gods? These are the gods who struck the Egyptians with all the plagues in the wilderness. [9] Be strong and conduct yourselves like men, you Philistines, that you do not become servants of the Hebrews, as they have been to you. Conduct yourselves like men, and fight!"

[10] So the Philistines fought, and Israel was defeated, and every man fled to his tent. There was a very great slaughter, and there fell of Israel thirty thousand foot soldiers. [11] Also the ark of God was captured; and the two sons of Eli, Hophni and Phinehas, died.

[12] Then a man of Benjamin ran from the battle line the same day, and came to Shiloh with his clothes torn and dirt on his head. [13] Now when he came, there was Eli, sitting on a seat by the wayside watching, for his heart trembled for the ark of God. And when the man came into the city and told it, all the city cried out. [14] When Eli heard the noise of the outcry, he said, "What does the sound of this tumult mean?" And the man came quickly and told Eli. [15] Eli was ninety-eight years old, and his eyes were so dim that he could not see.

[16] Then the man said to Eli, "I am he who came from the battle. And I fled today from the battle line."

And he said, "What happened, my son?"

[17] So the messenger answered and said, "Israel has fled before the Philistines, and there has been a great slaughter among the people. Also your two sons, Hophni and Phinehas, are dead; and the ark of God has been captured."

[18] Then it happened, when he made mention of the ark of God, that Eli fell off the seat backward by the side of the gate; and his neck was broken and he died, for the man was old and heavy. And he had judged Israel forty years.

EXPLORATION

1. The Israelites appear to have assumed that God would give them victory over the Philistines, even though there is no record that anyone inquired of the Lord before the battle. Why might they have believed that God would give them success?

---

2. What was the problem with the Israelites' decision to bring the ark into the battle?

---

3. What does this decision reveal that the people of Israel misunderstood about God?

---

4. What was the Philistines' reaction when they learned the ark of the covenant had come into the Hebrew camp?

_____

_____

_____

_____

5. The Israelites thought the ark would guarantee them success. What hard lesson did the people learn when the battle was over?

_____

_____

_____

_____

6. Remember the prophecy God had delivered through Samuel concerning Eli and his family. How was that prophecy fulfilled on this day?

_____

_____

_____

INSPIRATION

The ark of the covenant was a rectangular box commissioned by Moses. The chest was not large: three feet, nine inches tall and two feet, three inches wide. A trio of the most precious Hebrew artifacts indwelt the ark: a gold jar of unspoiled manna, Aaron's walking stick that had budded long after it was cut, and the precious stone tablets that had felt the engraving finger of God. A heavy golden plate, called the mercy seat, served as a lid to the chest.

Two cherubim of gold, with outstretched wings, faced each other and looked down on the golden lid. They represented the majesty of Jehovah watching over the law and the needs of the people. The ark symbolized God's provision (the manna), God's power (the staff), God's precepts (the commandments), and, most of all, God's presence.

When the Israelites suffered a defeat at the hands of the Philistines, they reasoned they could turn the tide of the next battle by bringing the ark into the fray. "Let us bring the ark of the LORD's covenant from Shiloh," they said, "so that he may go with us and save us from the hand of our enemies" (1 Samuel 4:3). They thought simply bringing the ark would assure God's presence and thus the victory. What they learned is that God comes on his own terms.

The Lord wasn't about to let his people believe they could manipulate his power. He wasn't some genie who popped out at the rub of a lamp or a butler who appeared at the ring of a bell. The outcome of the attempt was a sober reminder of this truth: "The Israelites were defeated and every man fled to his tent. The slaughter was very great; Israel lost thirty thousand foot soldiers. The ark of God was captured" (verses 10–11).

God comes, mind you. But he comes on his own terms. He comes when commands are revered, hearts are clean, and confession is made. As James wrote, "Wash your hands, you sinners, and purify your hearts, you double-minded.... Humble yourselves before the Lord, and he will lift you up" (James 4:8, 10). (From *Facing Your Giants* by Max Lucado.)

REACTION

7. The ark of the covenant symbolized God's provision, power, precepts, and presence. How has God demonstrated his provision, power, and presence to you?

----

8. What are some of the ways that God has revealed his precepts to you? What are some of the things the Lord has taught you recently about how to think and act?

9. The Israelites thought they could guarantee God's presence in battle by taking the ark into the fray. Why it is important to recognize that God comes on only his own terms?

10. When you think about the way you communicate with God in prayer, are you ever guilty of treating him like a genie who will grant your wishes? Explain your response.

11. What about treating the Lord like a butler who is ready to serve at your call? Have you ever been guilty of treating God that way? Explain your response.

12. God comes when commands are revered, hearts are clean, and confession is made. What do you need to do today to experience the presence of God?

_____

_____

_____

_____

_____

_____

_____

_____

_____

LIFE LESSONS

The Israelites in this story were under the mistaken belief that the ark _itself_ held special power. Much like the nations around them who trusted in "man-made gods of wood and stone" (Deuteronomy 4:28), they were placing their faith in a box made of wood and gold. The Lord revealed the error in his people's thinking by allowing them to not only lose to the Philistines but also to lose the ark. God revealed to the Israelites—just as he reveals to us today—that he is sovereign and acts according to his own plans and purposes . . . not to ours. As one biblical author succinctly put it, "The LORD does whatever pleases him" (Psalm 135:6).

DEVOTION

Lord, forgive us for any wrongful thinking on our part that you "owe" us anything or that we can compel you to do anything. We acknowledge that every breath we take and every day we spend on this earth is an act of your mercy. Teach us to be reverent and always humble before you.

JOURNALING

The capture of the ark challenged the Israelites' faulty belief that bringing it into battle would assure God's presence and protection. When is a time that God challenged a faulty belief that you were holding? What changed in your life after God revealed this to you?

FOR FURTHER READING

To complete the book of 1 Samuel during this twelve-part study, read 1 Samuel 4:1–7:17. For more Bible passages about God's sovereignty, read Job 42:2; Psalm 115:3; Proverbs 19:21; Daniel 4:35; Matthew 19:26; Luke 1:37; Romans 9:18; Revelation 4:11.

THE CRY FOR A KING

"No!" they said. "We want a king over us. Then
we will be like all the other nations."
1 Samuel 8:19–20

REFLECTION

What does it mean to truly make God the "king" over your life?

_____

_____

_____

_____

_____

_____

_____

_____

_____

_____

_____

_____

_____

SITUATION

The Philistines had captured the ark . . . but they soon began to regret it when the Lord afflicted them with plagues. The Philistines moved the ark from city to city before finally realizing they had no other choice but to send it back to the Israelites. The return of the ark brought about joy in Israel and also a return of the people's hearts to God. Samuel, seeing their sincerity, acted in his role as judge and led the Israelites to a great victory over the Philistines. Yet all was not well in the land, for Samuel's two sons began to abuse their power and act dishonestly. This caused concern for the elders of Israel, who recognized that Samuel was growing old and his sons would not be good successors. So they approached the prophet with a proposition.

OBSERVATION

*Read 1 Samuel 8:1–22 from the New International
Version or the New King James Version.*

NEW INTERNATIONAL VERSION

¹ When Samuel grew old, he appointed his sons as Israel's leaders. ² The name of his firstborn was Joel and the name of his second was Abijah, and they served at Beersheba. ³ But his sons did not follow his ways. They turned aside after dishonest gain and accepted bribes and perverted justice.

⁴ So all the elders of Israel gathered together and came to Samuel at Ramah. ⁵ They said to him, "You are old, and your sons do not follow your ways; now appoint a king to lead us, such as all the other nations have."

⁶ But when they said, "Give us a king to lead us," this displeased Samuel; so he prayed to the LORD. ⁷ And the LORD told him: "Listen to all that the people are saying to you; it is not you they have rejected, but they have rejected me as their king. ⁸ As they have done from the day I brought them up out of Egypt until this day, forsaking me and serving other gods, so they are doing to you. ⁹ Now listen to them; but warn them solemnly and let them know what the king who will reign over them will claim as his rights."

¹⁰ Samuel told all the words of the LORD to the people who were asking him for a king. ¹¹ He said, "This is what the king who will reign over you will claim as his rights: He will take your sons and make them serve with his chariots and horses, and they will run in front of his chariots. ¹² Some he will assign to be commanders of thousands and commanders of fifties, and others to plow his ground and reap his harvest, and still others to make weapons of war and equipment for his chariots. ¹³ He will take your daughters to be perfumers and cooks and bakers. ¹⁴ He will take the best of your fields and vineyards and olive groves and give them to his attendants. ¹⁵ He will take a tenth of your grain and of your vintage and give it to his officials and attendants. ¹⁶ Your male and female servants and the best of your cattle and donkeys he will take for his own use.

¹⁷ He will take a tenth of your flocks, and you yourselves will become his slaves. ¹⁸ When that day comes, you will cry out for relief from the king you have chosen, but the LORD will not answer you in that day."

¹⁹ But the people refused to listen to Samuel. "No!" they said. "We want a king over us. ²⁰ Then we will be like all the other nations, with a king to lead us and to go out before us and fight our battles."

²¹ When Samuel heard all that the people said, he repeated it before the LORD. ²² The LORD answered, "Listen to them and give them a king."

Then Samuel said to the Israelites, "Everyone go back to your own town."

NEW KING JAMES VERSION

¹ Now it came to pass when Samuel was old that he made his sons judges over Israel. ² The name of his firstborn was Joel, and the name of his second, Abijah; they were judges in Beersheba. ³ But his sons did not walk in his ways; they turned aside after dishonest gain, took bribes, and perverted justice.

⁴ Then all the elders of Israel gathered together and came to Samuel at Ramah, ⁵ and said to him, "Look, you are old, and your sons do not walk in your ways. Now make us a king to judge us like all the nations."

⁶ But the thing displeased Samuel when they said, "Give us a king to judge us." So Samuel prayed to the LORD. ⁷ And the LORD said to Samuel, "Heed the voice of the people in all that they say to you; for they have not rejected you, but they have rejected Me, that I should not reign over them. ⁸ According to all the works which they have done since the day that I brought them up out of Egypt, even to this day—with which they have forsaken Me and served other gods—so they are doing to you also. ⁹ Now therefore, heed their voice. However, you shall solemnly forewarn them, and show them the behavior of the king who will reign over them."

¹⁰ So Samuel told all the words of the LORD to the people who asked him for a king. ¹¹ And he said, "This will be the behavior of the king who will reign over you: He will take your sons and appoint them for his own chariots and to be his horsemen, and some will run before his chariots.

[12] He will appoint captains over his thousands and captains over his fifties, will set some to plow his ground and reap his harvest, and some to make his weapons of war and equipment for his chariots. [13] He will take your daughters to be perfumers, cooks, and bakers. [14] And he will take the best of your fields, your vineyards, and your olive groves, and give them to his servants. [15] He will take a tenth of your grain and your vintage, and give it to his officers and servants. [16] And he will take your male servants, your female servants, your finest young men, and your donkeys, and put them to his work. [17] He will take a tenth of your sheep. And you will be his servants. [18] And you will cry out in that day because of your king whom you have chosen for yourselves, and the LORD will not hear you in that day."

[19] Nevertheless the people refused to obey the voice of Samuel; and they said, "No, but we will have a king over us, [20] that we also may be like all the nations, and that our king may judge us and go out before us and fight our battles."

[21] And Samuel heard all the words of the people, and he repeated them in the hearing of the LORD. [22] So the LORD said to Samuel, "Heed their voice, and make them a king."

And Samuel said to the men of Israel, "Every man go to his city."

EXPLORATION

1. Samuel appointed his sons, Joel and Abijah, as leaders over Israel. What was the problem with this decision? In what ways were Samuel's sons like Eli's sons?

2. What reasons did the people give for wanting a king? Why do you think they were unsatisfied with being led by judges as God had designed?

_____

_____

_____

_____

3. Why was Samuel displeased with the people's request? What did the Lord say to him about the nature of his people when it came to wanting what other nations had?

_____

_____

_____

4. God instructed Samuel to warn the people about what a king would claim as his rights. What did Samuel say a king would demand from them in regard to their sons? What would the king demand from them when it came to their daughters?

_____

_____

_____

5. What did Samuel say a king would demand from the Israelites in regard to their fields, vineyards, and olive groves? What else would the king take from them?

_____

_____

_____

_____

6. Why did the people insist on having a king in spite of these warnings from Samuel? What does this reveal about their lack of trust in the Lord?

_____

_____

_____

_____

_____

_____

_____

_____

INSPIRATION

When God appeared to Abraham at the age of ninety-nine, the Lord promised that kings would come from his line: "I will make you very fruitful; I will make nations of you, and kings will come from you" (Genesis 17:6). He said the same of Abraham's wife, Sarah: "I will bless her so that she will be the mother of nations; kings of peoples will come from her" (verse 16). So what was the problem when the Israelites asked Samuel to appoint a king over them?

A clue can be found in the request: "Now appoint a king to lead us, *such as all the other nations have*" (1 Samuel 8:5, emphasis added). The Israelites were no longer interested in trusting God to lead them. They wanted a human king who would provide the symbol of strength they saw in the nations around them. They wanted to be like everyone else.

God wanted his people to be different. Not odd, or peculiar, but different in terms of being "set apart" from the world. The Lord had said to them, "Although the whole earth is mine, you will be for me a kingdom of priests and a holy nation" (Exodus 19:5–6). He had also told them, "Do not follow the crowd in doing wrong" (23:2).

Following the crowd can lead a person off the cliff. Just ask the Turkish shepherds who watched nearly fifteen hundred sheep do exactly that. For some undetermined reason, a single sheep jumped over the edge. The first was followed by a second, then a dozen, then several dozen. Pandemonium ensued. There was nothing the shepherds could do. Nearly one thousand five hundred animals jumped, and four hundred fifty died. The others would have perished as well, except that they landed on the bodies of the first jumpers.

Those sheep weren't thinking. If they were, they were saying to themselves, "Well, the jumpers look dumb. But a few hundred sheep can't be wrong, right?" Yes, they can. So can people. Don't copy the behavior and customs of this world. You cannot hear God if you are listening to them. You can't soar like an eagle if you are running with dumb sheep.

If you want to hear from the Lord, the first question you need to ask is not "What should I do?" but "Whom will I hear? Who has authority? Who calls the shots in my life?" If the answer is "people," you will not discern God's direction. If the answer is "television personalities," you will not discern God's will for your life. Add to that list horoscopes, palm readers, and tarot cards. If you are following the stars, you aren't following the Son. "The true children of God are those who let God's Spirit lead them" (Romans 8:14 NCV). (From *Help Is Here* by Max Lucado.)

REACTION

7. What advantages did the Israelites see in having a human king? What do you think was so attractive to the people about the fact that the nations around them had kings?

_____

_____

_____

_____

_____

_____

_____

_____

8. How do know when God is leading you in a direction that he wants you go? What does he make evident to help you know that he is the one doing the leading?

9. What does it look like, in practical terms, to reject God as your king?

10. When is a time you suffered the consequences of "following the crowd"? What did you learn through that experience about following your own path?

11. Why is it impossible to hear God if you are only listening to the voices of the people around you? When have you found this to be true in your life?

12. What is the problem in putting your faith in *anything* except the Lord God?

_____

_____

_____

_____

_____

_____

_____

_____

_____

LIFE LESSONS

The Lord had raised up Moses to lead the people out of Egypt. He had raised up Joshua to lead them into the promised land. He had raised up many other leaders—in the form of judges—to guide and protect them once they were established in the land. This was what God wanted for his people . . . with him as their king. But this is not what the people wanted. They wanted what all the other nations around them had—a *human* king—so they could be just like them. What they would learn is that it was dangerous to insist on getting their own way. God's ways may not seem as attractive as the world's ways, but in the end, they are always the *best* ways.

DEVOTION

Father, we are so often just like the Israelites. We want to be like everyone else in the world and are insistent on getting our own way. Forgive us for those times that we have rejected your authority. Help us to understand that you always have our best interests in mind.

JOURNALING

God, in an act of divine "tough love," allowed his people to have a king, even though he knew they would regret it. When is a time that God exhibited this same kind of tough love in your life? What did you learn about the perils of demanding your own way through that situation?

FOR FURTHER READING

To complete the book of 1 Samuel during this twelve-part study, read 1 Samuel 8:1–11:15. For more Bible passages about submitting to God, read 2 Chronicles 7:14; Job 22:21; Joel 2:13; Zephaniah 2:3; Matthew 23:12; Romans 8:7; James 4:7; 1 Peter 5:6.

OBEDIENCE IS BETTER THAN SACRIFICE

"To obey is better than sacrifice, and to heed is better than the fat of rams."
1 SAMUEL 15:22

REFLECTION

What are some of the ways in the past that you've tried to rationalize a bad decision you made?

_____

_____

_____

_____

_____

_____

_____

_____

_____

_____

_____

_____

SITUATION

In spite of God's warnings of what a king would bring, the people insisted on having a monarch. Israel would be a kingdom . . . and a man named Saul would be its first king. Saul was tall, handsome, and came from an influential Benjamite family. He seemed to be an ideal fit for what the people of Israel needed in a king—even though at first he was reluctant to take on the role. Saul's strength as a ruler was soon tested when the Ammonites besieged an Israelite town. Saul was successful in battle, leading to the people confirming him as their king. He then led the Israelites into a battle against the Philistines, which did not go as well. When his men began to desert, he grew nervous and made the first in a series of bad decisions.

OBSERVATION

Read 1 Samuel 13:5–15 and 15:10–23 from the
New International Version or the New King James Version.

New International Version

¹³:⁵ The Philistines assembled to fight Israel, with three thousand chariots, six thousand charioteers, and soldiers as numerous as the sand on the seashore. They went up and camped at Mikmash, east of Beth Aven. ⁶ When the Israelites saw that their situation was critical and that their army was hard pressed, they hid in caves and thickets, among the rocks, and in pits and cisterns. ⁷ Some Hebrews even crossed the Jordan to the land of Gad and Gilead.

Saul remained at Gilgal, and all the troops with him were quaking with fear. ⁸ He waited seven days, the time set by Samuel; but Samuel did not come to Gilgal, and Saul's men began to scatter. ⁹ So he said, "Bring me the burnt offering and the fellowship offerings." And Saul offered up the burnt offering. ¹⁰ Just as he finished making the offering, Samuel arrived, and Saul went out to greet him.

¹¹ "What have you done?" asked Samuel.

Saul replied, "When I saw that the men were scattering, and that you did not come at the set time, and that the Philistines were assembling at Mikmash, ¹² I thought, 'Now the Philistines will come down against me at Gilgal, and I have not sought the Lord's favor.' So I felt compelled to offer the burnt offering."

¹³ "You have done a foolish thing," Samuel said. "You have not kept the command the Lord your God gave you; if you had, he would have established your kingdom over Israel for all time. ¹⁴ But now your kingdom will not endure; the Lord has sought out a man after his own heart and appointed him ruler of his people, because you have not kept the Lord's command."

¹⁵ Then Samuel left Gilgal and went up to Gibeah in Benjamin, and Saul counted the men who were with him. They numbered about six hundred.

¹⁵:¹⁰ Then the word of the LORD came to Samuel: ¹¹ "I regret that I have made Saul king, because he has turned away from me and has not carried out my instructions." Samuel was angry, and he cried out to the LORD all that night.

¹² Early in the morning Samuel got up and went to meet Saul, but he was told, "Saul has gone to Carmel. There he has set up a monument in his own honor and has turned and gone on down to Gilgal."

¹³ When Samuel reached him, Saul said, "The LORD bless you! I have carried out the LORD's instructions."

¹⁴ But Samuel said, "What then is this bleating of sheep in my ears? What is this lowing of cattle that I hear?"

¹⁵ Saul answered, "The soldiers brought them from the Amalekites; they spared the best of the sheep and cattle to sacrifice to the LORD your God, but we totally destroyed the rest."

¹⁶ "Enough!" Samuel said to Saul. "Let me tell you what the LORD said to me last night."

"Tell me," Saul replied.

¹⁷ Samuel said, "Although you were once small in your own eyes, did you not become the head of the tribes of Israel? The LORD anointed you king over Israel. ¹⁸ And he sent you on a mission, saying, 'Go and completely destroy those wicked people, the Amalekites; wage war against them until you have wiped them out.' ¹⁹ Why did you not obey the LORD? Why did you pounce on the plunder and do evil in the eyes of the LORD?"

²⁰ "But I did obey the LORD," Saul said. "I went on the mission the LORD assigned me. I completely destroyed the Amalekites and brought back Agag their king. ²¹ The soldiers took sheep and cattle from the plunder, the best of what was devoted to God, in order to sacrifice them to the LORD your God at Gilgal."

²² But Samuel replied:

"Does the LORD delight in burnt offerings and sacrifices
    as much as in obeying the LORD?
To obey is better than sacrifice,

and to heed is better than the fat of rams.
²³ For rebellion is like the sin of divination,
    and arrogance like the evil of idolatry.
Because you have rejected the word of the Lord,
    he has rejected you as king."

New King James Version

^{13:5} Then the Philistines gathered together to fight with Israel, thirty thousand chariots and six thousand horsemen, and people as the sand which is on the seashore in multitude. And they came up and encamped in Michmash, to the east of Beth Aven. ⁶ When the men of Israel saw that they were in danger (for the people were distressed), then the people hid in caves, in thickets, in rocks, in holes, and in pits. ⁷ And some of the Hebrews crossed over the Jordan to the land of Gad and Gilead.

As for Saul, he was still in Gilgal, and all the people followed him trembling. ⁸ Then he waited seven days, according to the time set by Samuel. But Samuel did not come to Gilgal; and the people were scattered from him. ⁹ So Saul said, "Bring a burnt offering and peace offerings here to me." And he offered the burnt offering. ¹⁰ Now it happened, as soon as he had finished presenting the burnt offering, that Samuel came; and Saul went out to meet him, that he might greet him.

¹¹ And Samuel said, "What have you done?"

Saul said, "When I saw that the people were scattered from me, and that you did not come within the days appointed, and that the Philistines gathered together at Michmash, ¹² then I said, 'The Philistines will now come down on me at Gilgal, and I have not made supplication to the Lord.' Therefore I felt compelled, and offered a burnt offering."

¹³ And Samuel said to Saul, "You have done foolishly. You have not kept the commandment of the Lord your God, which He commanded you. For now the Lord would have established your kingdom over Israel forever. ¹⁴ But now your kingdom shall not continue. The Lord has sought for Himself a man after His own heart, and the Lord has

commanded him to be commander over His people, because you have not kept what the LORD commanded you."

15 Then Samuel arose and went up from Gilgal to Gibeah of Benjamin. And Saul numbered the people present with him, about six hundred men.

15:10 Now the word of the LORD came to Samuel, saying, 11 "I greatly regret that I have set up Saul as king, for he has turned back from following Me, and has not performed My commandments." And it grieved Samuel, and he cried out to the LORD all night. 12 So when Samuel rose early in the morning to meet Saul, it was told Samuel, saying, "Saul went to Carmel, and indeed, he set up a monument for himself; and he has gone on around, passed by, and gone down to Gilgal." 13 Then Samuel went to Saul, and Saul said to him, "Blessed are you of the LORD! I have performed the commandment of the LORD."

14 But Samuel said, "What then is this bleating of the sheep in my ears, and the lowing of the oxen which I hear?"

15 And Saul said, "They have brought them from the Amalekites; for the people spared the best of the sheep and the oxen, to sacrifice to the LORD your God; and the rest we have utterly destroyed."

16 Then Samuel said to Saul, "Be quiet! And I will tell you what the LORD said to me last night."

And he said to him, "Speak on."

17 So Samuel said, "When you were little in your own eyes, were you not head of the tribes of Israel? And did not the LORD anoint you king over Israel? 18 Now the LORD sent you on a mission, and said, 'Go, and utterly destroy the sinners, the Amalekites, and fight against them until they are consumed.' 19 Why then did you not obey the voice of the LORD? Why did you swoop down on the spoil, and do evil in the sight of the LORD?"

20 And Saul said to Samuel, "But I have obeyed the voice of the LORD, and gone on the mission on which the LORD sent me, and brought back Agag king of Amalek; I have utterly destroyed the Amalekites. 21 But the people took of the plunder, sheep and oxen, the best of the things which

should have been utterly destroyed, to sacrifice to the LORD your God in Gilgal."

²² So Samuel said:

> "Has the LORD as great delight in burnt offerings and sacrifices,
> As in obeying the voice of the LORD?
> Behold, to obey is better than sacrifice,
> And to heed than the fat of rams.
> ²³ For rebellion is as the sin of witchcraft,
> And stubbornness is as iniquity and idolatry.
> Because you have rejected the word of the LORD,
> He also has rejected you from being king."

EXPLORATION

1. The Israelites believed a king would give them greater confidence in battle. But what was the situation at the outset of the Israelites' battle with the Philistines?

_____

_____

_____

_____

_____

2. What impact did the state of the Israelite army have on Saul's decision to make the sacrifice? What impact did the delay in Samuel's arrival have on his decision?

_____

_____

_____

_____

3. What reasons did Saul give for proceeding with the sacrifice? What did Samuel say would happen because of Saul's disobedience to the Lord?

---

4. God instructed Saul to attack the Amalekites and utterly destroy all that they possessed. What did Saul do instead? How did he try to rationalize his decision?

---

5. Samuel pointed out that Saul had chosen to "pounce on the plunder" of the Amalekites (verse 19). What new excuse did Saul offer for why he had kept the sheep and cattle?

---

6. What did Samuel say the Lord wanted from King Saul above all else? What did Samuel reiterate would happen to Saul because of his repeated disobedience to God?

INSPIRATION

When Israel wanted a king, Samuel anointed one . . . Saul. The very name causes Samuel to groan. *Saul. Tall Saul. Strong Saul. The Israelites wanted a king, so we have a king. They wanted a leader, so we have . . . a louse.* Samuel glances from side to side, fearful that he may have spoken aloud what he intended only to think.

No one hears him. He's safe . . . as safe as you can be during the reign of a king gone manic. Saul's heart is growing harder, his eyes even wilder. He isn't the king he used to be.

One thousand BC was a bad era for this ramshackle collection of tribes called Israel. Joshua and Moses were history-class heroes. But three centuries of spiritual winter had now frozen the people's faith. One writer described the days between Joshua and Samuel with this terse sentence: "In those days Israel did not have a king. All the people did whatever seemed right in their own eyes" (Judges 21:25 NCV). Corruption fueled disruption. Immorality sired brutality.

The people had demanded a king. But rather than save the ship, Saul had nearly sunk it. Israel's first monarch turned out to be a blunderer. Not that it had started out that way. When Saul came to the throne, the Lord empowered him to win a great victory against the Ammonites (see 1 Samuel 11:1–11). But the next enemy Saul faced was more formidable: the Philistines. This warring, bloodthirsty, giant-breeding people monopolized iron and blacksmithing. They were grizzlies; Hebrews were salmon. Philistines built cities; Hebrews huddled in tents. Philistines forged iron weapons; Hebrews fought with crude slings and arrows. Philistines thundered in flashing chariots; Israelites retaliated with farm tools and knives.

When Saul saw his soldiers deserting, he grew nervous. God had told him to wait for Samuel before offering a sacrifice, but when the prophet didn't appear for seven days, Saul went ahead and offered it himself (see 13:5–15). The Lord gave Saul the victory in spite of his sin, and he enabled Saul to defeat the Israelites' next opponent: the Amalekites. Yet after the battle, Saul stumbled yet again. He disobeyed God's instruction through the prophet Samuel to completely destroy this people group and their king (see 15:10–22).

Corruption from within. Danger from without. Saul was weak, and the nation was weaker for it. What would God do? He would do what no one imagined—reject Saul as king and issue a surprise invitation for the job to a nobody from Nowheresville.

REACTION

7. Saul, at first, appeared to be everything the people wanted in a king. How have you likewise found that first impressions can be misleading when it comes to a person's character?

_____

_____

_____

_____

_____

_____

8. How would you describe what a "spiritual winter" looks like? When have you gone through such a cold and barren season in your life?

_____

_____

_____

_____

_____

_____

_____

9. Saul found it the most difficult to trust God when he saw his soldiers deserting. In what specific situations in your life do you find it the most difficult to trust God?

_____

_____

_____

_____

_____

10. Saul waited seven days for Samuel . . . and then determined to move ahead according to his own timetable. What do you find the most difficult about waiting on God's timing?

_____

_____

_____

_____

_____

11. Saul's act of disobedience when it came to the Amalekites was caused by his failure to resist the temptation to take plunder. How can you relate to Saul's struggle? What are some of the temptations the enemy throws at you to keep you from obeying God?

_____

_____

_____

_____

_____

12. What does Saul's story ultimately reveal about the cost of disobeying the Lord?

_____

_____

_____

_____

_____

_____

_____

_____

_____

LIFE LESSONS

Saul was willing to obey God as long as it suited his own plans and purposes. For instance, he was willing to follow God's instructions in attacking the Philistines because he knew this could lead to greater freedom for his people. But when the battle grew tense and his soldiers started deserting, he was unwilling to obey God and wait for Samuel to perform the sacrifice. Likewise, Saul was willing to attack the Amalekites and remove them as a threat. Yet he was unwilling to obey God's instruction to destroy all their possessions—because he wanted that wealth for himself. Saul's story reveals that we cannot obey God *in part*. We must obey him *completely*.

DEVOTION

Lord God, thank you for the warning that Saul's story provides to us. Keep our hearts from temptation. Keep our minds fully centered on you and your ways. We want to be people who are not just obedient in some areas of our lives but who are fully obedient to you.

JOURNALING

In what area of your life is God calling you to be fully obedient to him? What would it take for you to lay your will aside in that matter and completely follow God's will?

FOR FURTHER READING

To complete the book of 1 Samuel during this twelve-part study, read 1 Samuel 12:1–15:35. For more Bible passages about obeying God, read Exodus 19:5; Deuteronomy 28:1; Joshua 1:9; Isaiah 1:19; Luke 6:46; John 14:23; Romans 6:16; James 1:22.

GOD LOOKS AT THE HEART

*"People look at the outward appearance,
but the Lord looks at the heart."*
1 Samuel 16:7

REFLECTION

What are some of the ways that people have judged you in the past?

_____

_____

_____

_____

_____

_____

_____

_____

_____

_____

_____

_____

_____

SITUATION

The Lord had rejected Saul as king over Israel. Samuel, after proclaiming God's judgment, returned to his home in Ramah, and there he mourned for Saul. This went on until God said to him, "How long will you mourn for Saul, since I have rejected him as king over Israel?" (1 Samuel 16:1). The Lord then instructed Samuel to travel to the small village of Bethlehem, where he would anoint Saul's successor. Prophets were rarely seen in the town, and at first the elders—perhaps awed by Samuel's reputation—asked if he came in peace. Samuel responded that he had come to offer a sacrifice and then invited a man named Jesse and his sons to attend. It was during this "interview" that God would reveal his choice for who would be Israel's next king, though the decision would come as a great surprise to his prophet.

OBSERVATION

Read 1 Samuel 16:1–13 from the New International Version or the New King James Version.

New International Version

¹ The LORD said to Samuel, "How long will you mourn for Saul, since I have rejected him as king over Israel? Fill your horn with oil and be on your way; I am sending you to Jesse of Bethlehem. I have chosen one of his sons to be king."

² But Samuel said, "How can I go? If Saul hears about it, he will kill me."

The LORD said, "Take a heifer with you and say, 'I have come to sacrifice to the LORD.' ³ Invite Jesse to the sacrifice, and I will show you what to do. You are to anoint for me the one I indicate."

⁴ Samuel did what the LORD said. When he arrived at Bethlehem, the elders of the town trembled when they met him. They asked, "Do you come in peace?"

⁵ Samuel replied, "Yes, in peace; I have come to sacrifice to the LORD. Consecrate yourselves and come to the sacrifice with me." Then he consecrated Jesse and his sons and invited them to the sacrifice.

⁶ When they arrived, Samuel saw Eliab and thought, "Surely the LORD's anointed stands here before the LORD."

⁷ But the LORD said to Samuel, "Do not consider his appearance or his height, for I have rejected him. The LORD does not look at the things people look at. People look at the outward appearance, but the LORD looks at the heart."

⁸ Then Jesse called Abinadab and had him pass in front of Samuel. But Samuel said, "The LORD has not chosen this one either." ⁹ Jesse then had Shammah pass by, but Samuel said, "Nor has the LORD chosen this one." ¹⁰ Jesse had seven of his sons pass before Samuel, but Samuel said to him, "The LORD has not chosen these." ¹¹ So he asked Jesse, "Are these all the sons you have?"

"There is still the youngest," Jesse answered. "He is tending the sheep."

Samuel said, "Send for him; we will not sit down until he arrives."

¹² So he sent for him and had him brought in. He was glowing with health and had a fine appearance and handsome features.

Then the LORD said, "Rise and anoint him; this is the one."

¹³ So Samuel took the horn of oil and anointed him in the presence of his brothers, and from that day on the Spirit of the LORD came powerfully upon David. Samuel then went to Ramah.

NEW KING JAMES VERSION

¹ Now the LORD said to Samuel, "How long will you mourn for Saul, seeing I have rejected him from reigning over Israel? Fill your horn with oil, and go; I am sending you to Jesse the Bethlehemite. For I have provided Myself a king among his sons."

² And Samuel said, "How can I go? If Saul hears it, he will kill me."

But the LORD said, "Take a heifer with you, and say, 'I have come to sacrifice to the LORD.' ³ Then invite Jesse to the sacrifice, and I will show you what you shall do; you shall anoint for Me the one I name to you."

⁴ So Samuel did what the LORD said, and went to Bethlehem. And the elders of the town trembled at his coming, and said, "Do you come peaceably?"

⁵ And he said, "Peaceably; I have come to sacrifice to the LORD. Sanctify yourselves, and come with me to the sacrifice." Then he consecrated Jesse and his sons, and invited them to the sacrifice.

⁶ So it was, when they came, that he looked at Eliab and said, "Surely the LORD's anointed is before Him!"

⁷ But the LORD said to Samuel, "Do not look at his appearance or at his physical stature, because I have refused him. For the LORD does not see as man sees; for man looks at the outward appearance, but the LORD looks at the heart."

⁸ So Jesse called Abinadab, and made him pass before Samuel. And he said, "Neither has the LORD chosen this one." ⁹ Then Jesse made

Shammah pass by. And he said, "Neither has the LORD chosen this one." ¹⁰ Thus Jesse made seven of his sons pass before Samuel. And Samuel said to Jesse, "The LORD has not chosen these." ¹¹ And Samuel said to Jesse, "Are all the young men here?" Then he said, "There remains yet the youngest, and there he is, keeping the sheep."

And Samuel said to Jesse, "Send and bring him. For we will not sit down till he comes here." ¹² So he sent and brought him in. Now he was ruddy, with bright eyes, and good-looking. And the LORD said, "Arise, anoint him; for this is the one!" ¹³ Then Samuel took the horn of oil and anointed him in the midst of his brothers; and the Spirit of the LORD came upon David from that day forward. So Samuel arose and went to Ramah.

EXPLORATION

1. What was Samuel's concern in traveling to Bethlehem to meet with Jesse's sons?

2. How did God allay Samuel's fears? What was he to do when arrived in Bethlehem?

3. Why might the elders of Bethlehem have "trembled" when they saw Samuel in their town?

_____

_____

_____

_____

_____

4. When Samuel saw Eliab, he thought for sure that God would anoint him as king. How did the Lord respond to Samuel's thoughts about this son of Jesse?

_____

_____

_____

_____

_____

5. Why do you think Jesse didn't include David in the meeting with the prophet Samuel?

_____

_____

_____

_____

6. God often chooses those whom society overlooks or deems unworthy for his purposes. How do you see that reality play out in this story?

_____

_____

_____

_____

INSPIRATION

Samuel glances from side to side. His stomach churns and his thoughts race. It's hazardous to anoint a king when Israel already has one. Yet it's more hazardous to live with no leader in such explosive times. And so Samuel walks the trail toward Bethlehem.

The Bethlehem of Samuel's day was a sleepy village that time had forgotten, nestled in the foothills six miles south of Jerusalem. Bethlehem sat 2,000 feet above the Mediterranean, looking down on gentle, green hills that flattened into gaunt, rugged pastureland. Jesus would issue his first cry beneath Bethlehem's sky. But a thousand years before there will be a babe in a manger, Samuel enters the village, pulling a heifer.

His arrival turns the heads of the citizens. Prophets don't visit Bethlehem. Has he come to chastise someone or hide somewhere? Neither, the stoop-shouldered priest assures. He has come to sacrifice the animal to God and invites the elders and Jesse and his sons to join him.

The scene has a dog-show feel to it. Samuel examines the boys one at a time like canines on leashes, more than once ready to give the blue ribbon, but each time God stops him.

Eliab, the oldest, seems the logical choice. Envision him as the village Casanova: wavy-haired, strong-jawed. He wears tight jeans and has a piano-keyboard smile.

This is the guy, Samuel thinks. "Wrong," God says.

Abinadab enters as brother and contestant number two. You'd think a high-fashion model had just walked in. Italian suit. Alligator-skin shoes. Jet-black, oiled-back hair. Want a classy king? Abinadab has the bling-bling. But God's not into classy.

Samuel asks for brother number three, Shammah. He's bookish, studious. Could use a charisma transplant but busting with brains. Has a degree from State University and his eyes on a postgraduate program in Egypt. Jesse whispers, "Valedictorian of Bethlehem High." Samuel is impressed, but God isn't. He reminds his prophet, "People look at the outside of a person, but the Lord looks at the heart" (1 Samuel 16:7 NCV).

Seven sons pass. Seven sons fail. The procession comes to a halt. Samuel counts the siblings: *one, two, three, four, five, six . . . seven.* "Jesse, don't you have eight sons?" A similar question caused Cinderella's stepmother to squirm. Jesse likely did the same. "I still have the youngest son. He is out taking care of the sheep" (verse 11 NCV).

The Hebrew word for "youngest son" is *haqqaton*. It implies more than age; it suggests rank. Sheep-watching fits the family *haqqaton*. Put the boy where he can't cause trouble. Leave him with woolly heads and open skies.

And that's where we find David, in the pasture with the flock. Scripture dedicates sixty-six chapters to his story, more than anyone else in the Bible outside of Jesus. The New Testament mentions his name fifty-nine times. He will establish and inhabit the world's most famous city, Jerusalem. The Son of God will be called the Son of David. The greatest psalms will flow from his pen. We'll call him king, warrior, minstrel, and giant-killer.

But today he's not even included in the family meeting. He's just a forgotten, uncredentialed kid, performing a menial task in a map-dot town. Human eyes saw a gangly teenager enter the house, smelling like sheep and looking like he needed a bath. Yet the Lord said to Samuel, "Rise and anoint him; this is the one" (verse 12).

REACTION

7. God had given Samuel a difficult task: anoint a new king of Israel when the current king was still alive. What would you have been feeling if you were in Samuel's place?

----

8. When has God done something similar by asking you to move out of your comfort zone?

9. Samuel was impressed by Eliab's appearance and height. Why is it so easy to fall into the trap of believing that someone is a good fit for a role based solely on looks?

10. What characteristics do you look for in determining if someone is a good fit for a role?

11. David was not even invited by his father to appear before Samuel. How can you relate to his story? When is a moment in your life that you can recall feeling overlooked?

12. What does this story reveal about the characteristics in a person that are important to *God*? What does this story reveal when it comes to how he sees you?

_____

_____

_____

_____

_____

_____

_____

_____

_____

LIFE LESSONS

When the Israelites demanded a king, God gave them Saul. He was strong, from a well-to-do family, and was "a head taller than anyone else" (1 Samuel 9:2). It's an interesting detail, as typically only the height of Israel's enemies is mentioned in the Bible (see Numbers 13:22; Deuteronomy 9:2; 1 Samuel 17:4). The people had asked for a king "like all the nations" (1 Samuel 8:5 NKJV), and that is what they got. But when God chose David, he looked not at his outward appearance but on the inward condition of his heart. God wanted "a man after his own heart" (13:14). Today, he is still looking for those who seek after his own heart.

DEVOTION

Lord, we want to have the heart that David had toward you. We want to share the heart that you have for our world. Help us to not fall into the trap of putting up appearances of being "spiritual" to impress others. Let our motivations instead be based on your love for us.

JOURNALING

"People look at the outward appearance, but the LORD looks at the heart" (1 Samuel 16:7). When God looks at your heart today, what does he find? What do you *want* him to find?

FOR FURTHER READING

To complete the book of 1 Samuel during this twelve-part study, read
1 Samuel 16:1–23. For more Bible passages about God's plans for you,
read Psalm 37:23; 138:8; Proverbs 3:5–6; 16:9; Jeremiah 29:11; Ephesians
1:11; 2:10; Philippians 1:6.

A GIANT PROBLEM

"This day the Lord will deliver you into my hands."
1 Samuel 17:46

REFLECTION

When is the last time you faced an overwhelming problem that you knew you couldn't handle on your own? How did you see God move and provide for you in that situation?

_____

_____

_____

_____

_____

_____

_____

_____

_____

_____

_____

SITUATION

David had been anointed king of Israel, but that didn't mean he immediately stepped into the role. After all, Israel still had a king—though "the Spirit of the LORD had departed from Saul, and an evil spirit from the LORD tormented him" (1 Samuel 16:14). This led Saul's attendants to suggest that a musician come and play the lyre for the king whenever the evil spirit came over him. One servant knew just the person for the job: David, the son of Jesse. Soon, David was in the king's service, playing the lyre whenever he was needed, and traveling "back and forth from Saul to tend his father's sheep at Bethlehem" (17:15). It was during one of these times that David was back home that his father sent him to the Valley of Elah, where three of his brothers were fighting in the Israelite army against a formidable enemy led by a fear-inducing champion.

OBSERVATION

*Read 1 Samuel 17:1–58 from the New International
Version or the New King James Version.*

New International Version

¹ Now the Philistines gathered their forces for war and assembled at Sokoh in Judah. They pitched camp at Ephes Dammim, between Sokoh and Azekah. ² Saul and the Israelites assembled and camped in the Valley of Elah and drew up their battle line to meet the Philistines. ³ The Philistines occupied one hill and the Israelites another, with the valley between them.

⁴ A champion named Goliath, who was from Gath, came out of the Philistine camp. His height was six cubits and a span. ⁵ He had a bronze helmet on his head and wore a coat of scale armor of bronze weighing five thousand shekels; ⁶ on his legs he wore bronze greaves, and a bronze javelin was slung on his back. ⁷ His spear shaft was like a weaver's rod, and its iron point weighed six hundred shekels. His shield bearer went ahead of him.

⁸ Goliath stood and shouted to the ranks of Israel, "Why do you come out and line up for battle? Am I not a Philistine, and are you not the servants of Saul? Choose a man and have him come down to me. ⁹ If he is able to fight and kill me, we will become your subjects; but if I overcome him and kill him, you will become our subjects and serve us." ¹⁰ Then the Philistine said, "This day I defy the armies of Israel! Give me a man and let us fight each other." ¹¹ On hearing the Philistine's words, Saul and all the Israelites were dismayed and terrified.

¹² Now David was the son of an Ephrathite named Jesse, who was from Bethlehem in Judah. Jesse had eight sons, and in Saul's time he was very old. ¹³ Jesse's three oldest sons had followed Saul to the war: The firstborn was Eliab; the second, Abinadab; and the third, Shammah. ¹⁴ David was the youngest. The three oldest followed Saul, ¹⁵ but David went back and forth from Saul to tend his father's sheep at Bethlehem.

¹⁶ For forty days the Philistine came forward every morning and evening and took his stand.

¹⁷ Now Jesse said to his son David, "Take this ephah of roasted grain and these ten loaves of bread for your brothers and hurry to their camp. ¹⁸ Take along these ten cheeses to the commander of their unit. See how your brothers are and bring back some assurance from them. ¹⁹ They are with Saul and all the men of Israel in the Valley of Elah, fighting against the Philistines."

²⁰ Early in the morning David left the flock in the care of a shepherd, loaded up and set out, as Jesse had directed. He reached the camp as the army was going out to its battle positions, shouting the war cry. ²¹ Israel and the Philistines were drawing up their lines facing each other. ²² David left his things with the keeper of supplies, ran to the battle lines and asked his brothers how they were. ²³ As he was talking with them, Goliath, the Philistine champion from Gath, stepped out from his lines and shouted his usual defiance, and David heard it. ²⁴ Whenever the Israelites saw the man, they all fled from him in great fear.

²⁵ Now the Israelites had been saying, "Do you see how this man keeps coming out? He comes out to defy Israel. The king will give great wealth to the man who kills him. He will also give him his daughter in marriage and will exempt his family from taxes in Israel."

²⁶ David asked the men standing near him, "What will be done for the man who kills this Philistine and removes this disgrace from Israel? Who is this uncircumcised Philistine that he should defy the armies of the living God?"

²⁷ They repeated to him what they had been saying and told him, "This is what will be done for the man who kills him."

²⁸ When Eliab, David's oldest brother, heard him speaking with the men, he burned with anger at him and asked, "Why have you come down here? And with whom did you leave those few sheep in the wilderness? I know how conceited you are and how wicked your heart is; you came down only to watch the battle."

²⁹ "Now what have I done?" said David. "Can't I even speak?" ³⁰ He then turned away to someone else and brought up the same matter, and the men answered him as before. ³¹ What David said was overheard and reported to Saul, and Saul sent for him.

[32] David said to Saul, "Let no one lose heart on account of this Philistine; your servant will go and fight him."

[33] Saul replied, "You are not able to go out against this Philistine and fight him; you are only a young man, and he has been a warrior from his youth."

[34] But David said to Saul, "Your servant has been keeping his father's sheep. When a lion or a bear came and carried off a sheep from the flock, [35] I went after it, struck it and rescued the sheep from its mouth. When it turned on me, I seized it by its hair, struck it and killed it. [36] Your servant has killed both the lion and the bear; this uncircumcised Philistine will be like one of them, because he has defied the armies of the living God. [37] The LORD who rescued me from the paw of the lion and the paw of the bear will rescue me from the hand of this Philistine."

Saul said to David, "Go, and the LORD be with you."

[38] Then Saul dressed David in his own tunic. He put a coat of armor on him and a bronze helmet on his head. [39] David fastened on his sword over the tunic and tried walking around, because he was not used to them.

"I cannot go in these," he said to Saul, "because I am not used to them." So he took them off. [40] Then he took his staff in his hand, chose five smooth stones from the stream, put them in the pouch of his shepherd's bag and, with his sling in his hand, approached the Philistine.

[41] Meanwhile, the Philistine, with his shield bearer in front of him, kept coming closer to David. [42] He looked David over and saw that he was little more than a boy, glowing with health and handsome, and he despised him. [43] He said to David, "Am I a dog, that you come at me with sticks?" And the Philistine cursed David by his gods. [44] "Come here," he said, "and I'll give your flesh to the birds and the wild animals!"

[45] David said to the Philistine, "You come against me with sword and spear and javelin, but I come against you in the name of the LORD Almighty, the God of the armies of Israel, whom you have defied. [46] This day the LORD will deliver you into my hands, and I'll strike you down and cut off your head. This very day I will give the carcasses of the Philistine army to the birds and the wild animals, and the whole world will know

that there is a God in Israel. ⁴⁷ All those gathered here will know that it is not by sword or spear that the LORD saves; for the battle is the LORD's, and he will give all of you into our hands."

⁴⁸ As the Philistine moved closer to attack him, David ran quickly toward the battle line to meet him. ⁴⁹ Reaching into his bag and taking out a stone, he slung it and struck the Philistine on the forehead. The stone sank into his forehead, and he fell facedown on the ground.

⁵⁰ So David triumphed over the Philistine with a sling and a stone; without a sword in his hand he struck down the Philistine and killed him.

⁵¹ David ran and stood over him. He took hold of the Philistine's sword and drew it from the sheath. After he killed him, he cut off his head with the sword.

When the Philistines saw that their hero was dead, they turned and ran. ⁵² Then the men of Israel and Judah surged forward with a shout and pursued the Philistines to the entrance of Gath and to the gates of Ekron. Their dead were strewn along the Shaaraim road to Gath and Ekron. ⁵³ When the Israelites returned from chasing the Philistines, they plundered their camp.

⁵⁴ David took the Philistine's head and brought it to Jerusalem; he put the Philistine's weapons in his own tent.

⁵⁵ As Saul watched David going out to meet the Philistine, he said to Abner, commander of the army, "Abner, whose son is that young man?"

Abner replied, "As surely as you live, Your Majesty, I don't know."

⁵⁶ The king said, "Find out whose son this young man is."

⁵⁷ As soon as David returned from killing the Philistine, Abner took him and brought him before Saul, with David still holding the Philistine's head.

⁵⁸ "Whose son are you, young man?" Saul asked him.

David said, "I am the son of your servant Jesse of Bethlehem."

NEW KING JAMES VERSION

¹ Now the Philistines gathered their armies together to battle, and were gathered at Sochoh, which belongs to Judah; they encamped between

Sochoh and Azekah, in Ephes Dammim. ² And Saul and the men of Israel were gathered together, and they encamped in the Valley of Elah, and drew up in battle array against the Philistines. ³ The Philistines stood on a mountain on one side, and Israel stood on a mountain on the other side, with a valley between them.

⁴ And a champion went out from the camp of the Philistines, named Goliath, from Gath, whose height was six cubits and a span. ⁵ He had a bronze helmet on his head, and he was armed with a coat of mail, and the weight of the coat was five thousand shekels of bronze. ⁶ And he had bronze armor on his legs and a bronze javelin between his shoulders. ⁷ Now the staff of his spear was like a weaver's beam, and his iron spear-head weighed six hundred shekels; and a shield-bearer went before him. ⁸ Then he stood and cried out to the armies of Israel, and said to them, "Why have you come out to line up for battle? Am I not a Philistine, and you the servants of Saul? Choose a man for yourselves, and let him come down to me. ⁹ If he is able to fight with me and kill me, then we will be your servants. But if I prevail against him and kill him, then you shall be our servants and serve us." ¹⁰ And the Philistine said, "I defy the armies of Israel this day; give me a man, that we may fight together." ¹¹ When Saul and all Israel heard these words of the Philistine, they were dismayed and greatly afraid.

¹² Now David was the son of that Ephrathite of Bethlehem Judah, whose name was Jesse, and who had eight sons. And the man was old, advanced in years, in the days of Saul. ¹³ The three oldest sons of Jesse had gone to follow Saul to the battle. The names of his three sons who went to the battle were Eliab the firstborn, next to him Abinadab, and the third Shammah. ¹⁴ David was the youngest. And the three oldest followed Saul. ¹⁵ But David occasionally went and returned from Saul to feed his father's sheep at Bethlehem.

¹⁶ And the Philistine drew near and presented himself forty days, morning and evening.

¹⁷ Then Jesse said to his son David, "Take now for your brothers an ephah of this dried grain and these ten loaves, and run to your brothers

at the camp. ¹⁸ And carry these ten cheeses to the captain of their thousand, and see how your brothers fare, and bring back news of them." ¹⁹ Now Saul and they and all the men of Israel were in the Valley of Elah, fighting with the Philistines.

²⁰ So David rose early in the morning, left the sheep with a keeper, and took the things and went as Jesse had commanded him. And he came to the camp as the army was going out to the fight and shouting for the battle. ²¹ For Israel and the Philistines had drawn up in battle array, army against army. ²² And David left his supplies in the hand of the supply keeper, ran to the army, and came and greeted his brothers. ²³ Then as he talked with them, there was the champion, the Philistine of Gath, Goliath by name, coming up from the armies of the Philistines; and he spoke according to the same words. So David heard them. ²⁴ And all the men of Israel, when they saw the man, fled from him and were dreadfully afraid. ²⁵ So the men of Israel said, "Have you seen this man who has come up? Surely he has come up to defy Israel; and it shall be that the man who kills him the king will enrich with great riches, will give him his daughter, and give his father's house exemption from taxes in Israel."

²⁶ Then David spoke to the men who stood by him, saying, "What shall be done for the man who kills this Philistine and takes away the reproach from Israel? For who is this uncircumcised Philistine, that he should defy the armies of the living God?"

²⁷ And the people answered him in this manner, saying, "So shall it be done for the man who kills him."

²⁸ Now Eliab his oldest brother heard when he spoke to the men; and Eliab's anger was aroused against David, and he said, "Why did you come down here? And with whom have you left those few sheep in the wilderness? I know your pride and the insolence of your heart, for you have come down to see the battle."

²⁹ And David said, "What have I done now? Is there not a cause?" ³⁰ Then he turned from him toward another and said the same thing; and these people answered him as the first ones did.

[31] Now when the words which David spoke were heard, they reported them to Saul; and he sent for him. [32] Then David said to Saul, "Let no man's heart fail because of him; your servant will go and fight with this Philistine."

[33] And Saul said to David, "You are not able to go against this Philistine to fight with him; for you are a youth, and he a man of war from his youth."

[34] But David said to Saul, "Your servant used to keep his father's sheep, and when a lion or a bear came and took a lamb out of the flock, [35] I went out after it and struck it, and delivered the lamb from its mouth; and when it arose against me, I caught it by its beard, and struck and killed it. [36] Your servant has killed both lion and bear; and this uncircumcised Philistine will be like one of them, seeing he has defied the armies of the living God." [37] Moreover David said, "The LORD, who delivered me from the paw of the lion and from the paw of the bear, He will deliver me from the hand of this Philistine."

And Saul said to David, "Go, and the LORD be with you!"

[38] So Saul clothed David with his armor, and he put a bronze helmet on his head; he also clothed him with a coat of mail. [39] David fastened his sword to his armor and tried to walk, for he had not tested them. And David said to Saul, "I cannot walk with these, for I have not tested them." So David took them off.

[40] Then he took his staff in his hand; and he chose for himself five smooth stones from the brook, and put them in a shepherd's bag, in a pouch which he had, and his sling was in his hand. And he drew near to the Philistine. [41] So the Philistine came, and began drawing near to David, and the man who bore the shield went before him. [42] And when the Philistine looked about and saw David, he disdained him; for he was only a youth, ruddy and good-looking. [43] So the Philistine said to David, "Am I a dog, that you come to me with sticks?" And the Philistine cursed David by his gods. [44] And the Philistine said to David, "Come to me, and I will give your flesh to the birds of the air and the beasts of the field!"

⁴⁵ Then David said to the Philistine, "You come to me with a sword, with a spear, and with a javelin. But I come to you in the name of the LORD of hosts, the God of the armies of Israel, whom you have defied. ⁴⁶ This day the LORD will deliver you into my hand, and I will strike you and take your head from you. And this day I will give the carcasses of the camp of the Philistines to the birds of the air and the wild beasts of the earth, that all the earth may know that there is a God in Israel. ⁴⁷ Then all this assembly shall know that the LORD does not save with sword and spear; for the battle is the LORD's, and He will give you into our hands."

⁴⁸ So it was, when the Philistine arose and came and drew near to meet David, that David hurried and ran toward the army to meet the Philistine. ⁴⁹ Then David put his hand in his bag and took out a stone; and he slung it and struck the Philistine in his forehead, so that the stone sank into his forehead, and he fell on his face to the earth. ⁵⁰ So David prevailed over the Philistine with a sling and a stone, and struck the Philistine and killed him. But there was no sword in the hand of David. ⁵¹ Therefore David ran and stood over the Philistine, took his sword and drew it out of its sheath and killed him, and cut off his head with it.

And when the Philistines saw that their champion was dead, they fled. ⁵² Now the men of Israel and Judah arose and shouted, and pursued the Philistines as far as the entrance of the valley and to the gates of Ekron. And the wounded of the Philistines fell along the road to Shaaraim, even as far as Gath and Ekron. ⁵³ Then the children of Israel returned from chasing the Philistines, and they plundered their tents. ⁵⁴ And David took the head of the Philistine and brought it to Jerusalem, but he put his armor in his tent.

⁵⁵ When Saul saw David going out against the Philistine, he said to Abner, the commander of the army, "Abner, whose son is this youth?"

And Abner said, "As your soul lives, O king, I do not know."

⁵⁶ So the king said, "Inquire whose son this young man is."

⁵⁷ Then, as David returned from the slaughter of the Philistine, Abner took him and brought him before Saul with the head of the Philistine in his hand. ⁵⁸ And Saul said to him, "Whose son are you, young man?"

So David answered, "I am the son of your servant Jesse the Bethlehemite."

EXPLORATION

1. Goliath is described as a giant of a man who was the Philistines' "champion" (verse 4). What was Goliath's challenge? What proposition did he make to the Israelites?

_____

_____

_____

_____

_____

2. How did the Israelites react whenever they saw Goliath? How did David react when he arrived on the scene and heard the giant's taunts?

_____

_____

_____

_____

3. Why do think Eliab "burned with anger" when he heard David speaking with the men (verse 28)? What was Eliab's impression of his younger brother?

_____

_____

_____

_____

4. What qualifications did David give to Saul as to why he was prepared to fight Goliath? What made David confident he would defeat the giant?

_____

_____

_____

_____

5. How did David respond to Goliath's taunts? What did David say the whole world would come to understand after he had defeated Goliath?

_____

_____

_____

_____

6. Why did David refuse to take the weapons and armor that Saul wanted to give to him? How might the battle have gone differently if he had accepted them?

_____

_____

_____

_____

INSPIRATION

David just showed up this morning. He clocked out of sheep-watching to deliver bread and cheese to his brothers on the battlefront. That's where David hears Goliath defying God, and that's when David makes his decision. Then he takes his staff in his hand and chooses five smooth stones from the brook. He puts them in a shepherd's bag, in a pouch that he has, and his sling is in his hand. And he draws near to the Philistine.

Goliath scoffs at the kid, nicknames him Twiggy. "Am I a dog, that you come to me with sticks?" (1 Samuel 17:43 NASB). Skinny, scrawny David. Bulky, brutish Goliath. The toothpick versus the tornado. The minibike attacking the eighteen-wheeler. The toy poodle taking on the rottweiler. What odds do you give David against his giant?

Better odds, perhaps, than you give yourself against yours. Your Goliath doesn't carry a sword or a shield; he brandishes blades of unemployment, abandonment, sexual abuse, or depression. Your giant doesn't parade up and down the hills of Elah; he prances through your office, your bedroom, your classroom. He brings bills you can't pay, grades you can't make, people you can't please, whiskey you can't resist, pornography you can't refuse, a career you can't escape, a past you can't shake, and a future you can't face.

You know well the roar of Goliath. You recognize his walk and wince at his talk. The question is—is he all you see? You know his voice—but is it all you hear? David saw and heard more. Read the first words he spoke, not just in the battle, but in the Bible: "What will be done for the man who kills this Philistine and removes this disgrace from Israel? Who is this uncircumcised Philistine that he should defy the armies of the living God?" (verse 26).

No one else discusses God. David discusses no one else but God. A subplot appears in the story. More than "David versus Goliath," this is "God-focus versus giant-focus."

David spots the target and seizes the moment. The sound of the swirling sling is the only sound in the valley. *Ssshhhww. Ssshhhww. Ssshhhww.* The stone torpedoes through the air and into the skull; Goliath's eyes cross and his legs buckle. He crumples to the ground and dies.

When was the last time you rushed your giant like David did in this story? *Giant of divorce, you aren't entering my home! Giant of depression? It may take a lifetime, but you won't conquer me. Giant of alcohol, bigotry, child abuse, insecurity . . . you're going down.* How long since you loaded your sling and took a swing at your giant?

Giants. We must face them. Yet we do not need to face them alone. Focus first, and most, on the Lord. The God who made a miracle out of David stands ready to make one out of you. (From *Facing Your Giants* by Max Lucado.)

REACTION

7. "Goliaths" in life come in many different forms. What is your Goliath right now—the biggest challenge or struggle that you are facing?

8. Goliath taunted the Israelites morning and evening. What are some of the ways that your Goliath taunts you throughout the day?

9. David focused not on Goliath but on what he knew about the character of God. What helps you to maintain your "God focus" like David?

10. Part of the reason as to why David was confident that God was with him in the present is because God had been with him in the past. How have you seen God's presence with you in the past? How can this help you to better face your Goliaths in the present?

11. When was the last time you rushed your Goliath like David did? What, if anything, is preventing you from taking a swing at your giant?

---

12. What reassurance does David's story provide that God will be with you when you face your Goliath? Where do you most need to feel his presence today?

LIFE LESSONS

When David agreed to step onto the battlefield with Goliath, it wasn't because he trusted in his skills with the sling. Nor did he agree to fight the giant based on any delusions that he could prevail in his own strength. No, David was able to courageously step onto the battlefield only because he knew that *God* was with him. David understood the battle belonged to the Lord, which is why he could say to Goliath, "This day the LORD will deliver you into my hands" (1 Samuel 17:46). We can have the same confidence in the battles against our own giants, knowing that God "gives us the victory through our Lord Jesus Christ" (1 Corinthians 15:57).

DEVOTION

Lord, we ask that you give us your strength today in the battle against our giants. Please give us the courage we need to step into the fray and overcome the challenges that seek to overwhelm us. May we always keep our eyes on you and understand the victory you have given us in Christ.

JOURNALING

"David triumphed over the Philistine with a sling and a stone" (1 Samuel 17:50). What resources has God provided to you to fight your Goliath that you might be overlooking?

FOR FURTHER READING

To complete the book of 1 Samuel during this twelve-part study, read 1 Samuel 17:1–58. For more Bible passages about relying on God's strength, read Exodus 15:2; 1 Chronicles 16:11; Psalm 20:7; Isaiah 41:10; 2 Corinthians 12:9; Ephesians 6:10; Philippians 4:13; 2 Timothy 1:7.

THE PROBLEM WITH POPULARITY

"They have credited David with tens of thousands,"
[Saul] thought, "but me with only thousands.
What more can he get but the kingdom?"
1 SAMUEL 18:8

REFLECTION

How do you seek to congratulate and build up your friends when they experience success?

_____

_____

_____

_____

_____

_____

_____

_____

_____

_____

_____

_____

_____

_____

_____

SITUATION

David had already been brought into Saul's service before the battle with Goliath, traveling from Bethlehem to play the lyre whenever the evil spirit came over the king, but his victory over the Philistine giant elevated his status to a new level. Abner, the commander of the Israelite army, brought David before Saul after the victory, and from that day on David stayed with the king. It was also at this time that David met Jonathan, the firstborn son of Saul who was in line for succession . . . though God had already chosen David to be Israel's next king. David quickly found success in whatever mission that Saul sent him on, and he rose in rank in the army. However, the popularity this brought soon caused problems for David.

OBSERVATION

Read 1 Samuel 18:1–16 from the New International
Version or the New King James Version.

NEW INTERNATIONAL VERSION

¹ After David had finished talking with Saul, Jonathan became one in spirit with David, and he loved him as himself. ² From that day Saul kept David with him and did not let him return home to his family. ³ And Jonathan made a covenant with David because he loved him as himself. ⁴ Jonathan took off the robe he was wearing and gave it to David, along with his tunic, and even his sword, his bow and his belt.

⁵ Whatever mission Saul sent him on, David was so successful that Saul gave him a high rank in the army. This pleased all the troops, and Saul's officers as well.

⁶ When the men were returning home after David had killed the Philistine, the women came out from all the towns of Israel to meet King Saul with singing and dancing, with joyful songs and with timbrels and lyres. ⁷ As they danced, they sang:

> "Saul has slain his thousands,
>   and David his tens of thousands."

⁸ Saul was very angry; this refrain displeased him greatly. "They have credited David with tens of thousands," he thought, "but me with only thousands. What more can he get but the kingdom?" ⁹ And from that time on Saul kept a close eye on David.

¹⁰ The next day an evil spirit from God came forcefully on Saul. He was prophesying in his house, while David was playing the lyre, as he usually did. Saul had a spear in his hand ¹¹ and he hurled it, saying to himself, "I'll pin David to the wall." But David eluded him twice.

¹² Saul was afraid of David, because the LORD was with David but had departed from Saul. ¹³ So he sent David away from him and gave

him command over a thousand men, and David led the troops in their campaigns. ¹⁴ In everything he did he had great success, because the LORD was with him. ¹⁵ When Saul saw how successful he was, he was afraid of him. ¹⁶ But all Israel and Judah loved David, because he led them in their campaigns.

NEW KING JAMES VERSION

¹ Now when he had finished speaking to Saul, the soul of Jonathan was knit to the soul of David, and Jonathan loved him as his own soul. ² Saul took him that day, and would not let him go home to his father's house anymore. ³ Then Jonathan and David made a covenant, because he loved him as his own soul. ⁴ And Jonathan took off the robe that was on him and gave it to David, with his armor, even to his sword and his bow and his belt.

⁵ So David went out wherever Saul sent him, and behaved wisely. And Saul set him over the men of war, and he was accepted in the sight of all the people and also in the sight of Saul's servants. ⁶ Now it had happened as they were coming home, when David was returning from the slaughter of the Philistine, that the women had come out of all the cities of Israel, singing and dancing, to meet King Saul, with tambourines, with joy, and with musical instruments. ⁷ So the women sang as they danced, and said:

> "Saul has slain his thousands,
> And David his ten thousands."

⁸ Then Saul was very angry, and the saying displeased him; and he said, "They have ascribed to David ten thousands, and to me they have ascribed only thousands. Now what more can he have but the kingdom?" ⁹ So Saul eyed David from that day forward.

¹⁰ And it happened on the next day that the distressing spirit from God came upon Saul, and he prophesied inside the house. So David played music with his hand, as at other times; but there was a spear in

Saul's hand. [11] And Saul cast the spear, for he said, "I will pin David to the wall!" But David escaped his presence twice.

[12] Now Saul was afraid of David, because the LORD was with him, but had departed from Saul. [13] Therefore Saul removed him from his presence, and made him his captain over a thousand; and he went out and came in before the people. [14] And David behaved wisely in all his ways, and the LORD was with him. [15] Therefore, when Saul saw that he behaved very wisely, he was afraid of him. [16] But all Israel and Judah loved David, because he went out and came in before them.

EXPLORATION

1. How is the friendship between David and Jonathan described in this passage?

2. David had refused to take the armor offered by Saul in his fight against Goliath. Why do you think he now readily accepted the tunic, sword, bow, and belt from Jonathan?

3. What was Saul's initial reaction to David's success in battle? What caused him to change and start suspecting David of usurping his throne?

4. What is the reason given as to why Saul suddenly threw a spear at David? What reason is provided as to why Saul grew afraid of David?

5. What was Saul's motivation in offering his daughters Merab and then Michal to David? Why might Saul have been so interested in making David his son-in-law?

6. What was Saul's plot in setting the dowry for his daughter Michal's hand in marriage? How did David respond to this challenge?

INSPIRATION

Poor David. The Valley of Elah proved to be boot camp for the king's court. When Goliath lost his head, the Hebrews made David their hero. People threw him a ticker-tape parade and sang, "Saul has slain his thousands, and David his tens of thousands" (1 Samuel 18:7).

Saul explodes like the Vesuvius he is. He eyes David "from that day forward" (verse 9 NKJV). The king is already a troubled soul, prone to angry eruptions, mad enough to eat bees. David's popularity splashes gasoline on Saul's temper. "I'll pin David to the wall" (verse 11).

Saul tries to kill Bethlehem's golden boy six different times. First, he invites David to marry his daughter Michal. Seems like a kind gesture, until you read the crude dowry Saul required: one hundred Philistine foreskins. *Surely one of the Philistines will kill David*, Saul hopes. They don't. David doubles the demand and returns with the proof.

Saul doesn't give up. He orders his servants and Jonathan to kill David, but they refuse. He tries with the spear another time but misses. Saul sends messengers to David's house to kill him, but his wife, Michal, lowers him through a window.

Saul's anger puzzles David. What has he done but good? He has brought musical healing to Saul's tortured spirit, hope to the enfeebled nation. He is the Abraham Lincoln of the Hebrew calamity, saving the republic and doing so modestly and honestly. He behaves "wisely in all his ways" (verse 14 NKJV). "All Israel and Judah loved David" (verse 16). David behaves "more wisely than all the servants of Saul, so that his name became highly esteemed" (verse 30 NKJV).

Yet Mount Saul keeps erupting, rewarding David's deeds with flying spears and murder plots. We understand David's question to Jonathan: "What have I done? What is my crime? How have I wronged your father, that he is trying to kill me?" (20:1).

Jonathan has no answer to give, for no answer exists. Who can justify the rage of a Saul? Who knows why a father torments a child, a wife belittles her husband, a boss pits employees against each other? But they do. Sauls still rage on our planet. Dictators torture, employers seduce, ministers abuse, priests molest, the strong and mighty control and cajole the vulnerable and innocent. Sauls still stalk Davids.

How does God respond in such cases? Nuke the nemesis? We may want him to do so. He has been known to extract a few Herods and Pharaohs. How he will treat yours, I can't say. But how he will treat you, I can. He will send you a Jonathan.

God counters Saul's cruelty with Jonathan's loyalty. Jonathan had reason to despise David, but he didn't. He was gracious. Gracious because the hand of the Master Weaver took his and David's hearts and stitched a seam between them. "Jonathan became one in spirit with David, and he loved him as himself" (18:1). (From *Facing Your Giants* by Max Lucado.)

REACTION

7. Paul instructed followers of Jesus to "rejoice with those who rejoice" (Romans 12:15). How well do you rejoice with others when they experience success?

---

8. How comfortable are you in sharing your victories with friends, family, and loved ones? Do you ever have concerns about how they will react? Explain your response.

---

9. Life comes with Goliaths . . . and also with Sauls. Who or what represents a "raging Saul" in your life? What problems has that raging Saul been causing you?

10. Fortunately, life also comes with "Jonathans" . . . those true friends who walk with you through the struggle and strife. Who are some of the Jonathans in your life?

11. What has that person done that has helped you deal with your raging Saul? How have you seen God's grace and mercy to you through that person's actions?

12. What are some other ways that God has provided comfort to you in difficult situations?

_____

_____

_____

_____

_____

_____

_____

LIFE LESSONS

The reaction to David's popularity between father and son could not have been more different. Saul kept close watch on David. He hurled spears at him. He sent David on missions where he was sure that he would die. He married David to his daughter Michal "so that she [might] be a snare to him" (1 Samuel 18:21). He did everything he could to protect the throne for his family. Jonathan, on the other hand, gave David the robe of a prince. He handed over his own sword, bow, and belt. Jonathan, the heir to the throne, effectively surrendered the throne to David. "You will be king over Israel," he later said, "and I will be second to you" (23:17). Jonathan esteemed God's choice for Israel's king over his own self-interests. This is what God calls us to do in our world today. As the apostle Paul wrote, "Do nothing out of selfish ambition or vain conceit. Rather, in humility value others above yourselves" (Philippians 2:3).

DEVOTION

Heavenly Father, we desire to treat others in a way that is honoring and loving toward them. We pray that you will keep us from envy and jealousy toward those who have received your blessings. Show us how to practice humility and value the people in our lives above ourselves.

JOURNALING

James wrote, "Humble yourselves before the Lord, and he will life you up" (James 4:10). What struggles do you have when it comes to showing humility? What are three practical steps that you could take today to become a person who values others above yourself?

FOR FURTHER READING

To complete the book of 1 Samuel during this twelve-part study, read 1 Samuel 18:1–30. For more Bible passages about humility, read Proverbs 11:2; 22:4; 2 Chronicles 7:14; Micah 6:8; Luke 14:11; Colossians 3:12; James 4:10; 1 Peter 1:5.

LIVING IN DESPERATE DAYS

"Now then, what do you have on hand? Give me five loaves of bread, or whatever you can find."

1 SAMUEL 21:3

REFLECTION

What are some of the ways that you like to help out people when you see that they are in need?

_____

_____

_____

_____

_____

_____

_____

_____

_____

_____

_____

_____

_____

_____

_____

_____

_____

_____

SITUATION

Saul's plans to get rid of David had come to nothing. David had dodged the spears that Saul threw at him on two occasions. He had prevailed over the Philistines when Saul demanded one hundred enemy foreskins as a dowry for his daughter Michal. "When Saul realized that the LORD was with David and that his daughter Michal loved David, Saul became still more afraid of him" (1 Samuel 18:28–29). This fear provoked Saul to instruct Jonathan and his attendants to kill David. "But Jonathan had taken a great liking to David" (19:1), so instead of trying to kill David, he warned him of the plot. Jonathan even offered to speak with his father on David's behalf to negotiate peace between the men. Saul would agree to his son's request . . . but then quickly go back to his murderous plots.

OBSERVATION

Read 1 Samuel 19:4–10 and 21:1–15 from the
New International Version or the New King James Version.

New International Version

^{19:4} Jonathan spoke well of David to Saul his father and said to him, "Let not the king do wrong to his servant David; he has not wronged you, and what he has done has benefited you greatly. ⁵ He took his life in his hands when he killed the Philistine. The LORD won a great victory for all Israel, and you saw it and were glad. Why then would you do wrong to an innocent man like David by killing him for no reason?"

⁶ Saul listened to Jonathan and took this oath: "As surely as the LORD lives, David will not be put to death."

⁷ So Jonathan called David and told him the whole conversation. He brought him to Saul, and David was with Saul as before.

⁸ Once more war broke out, and David went out and fought the Philistines. He struck them with such force that they fled before him.

⁹ But an evil spirit from the LORD came on Saul as he was sitting in his house with his spear in his hand. While David was playing the lyre, ¹⁰ Saul tried to pin him to the wall with his spear, but David eluded him as Saul drove the spear into the wall. That night David made good his escape.

^{21:1} David went to Nob, to Ahimelek the priest. Ahimelek trembled when he met him, and asked, "Why are you alone? Why is no one with you?"

² David answered Ahimelek the priest, "The king sent me on a mission and said to me, 'No one is to know anything about the mission I am

sending you on.' As for my men, I have told them to meet me at a certain place. ³ Now then, what do you have on hand? Give me five loaves of bread, or whatever you can find."

⁴ But the priest answered David, "I don't have any ordinary bread on hand; however, there is some consecrated bread here—provided the men have kept themselves from women."

⁵ David replied, "Indeed women have been kept from us, as usual whenever I set out. The men's bodies are holy even on missions that are not holy. How much more so today!" ⁶ So the priest gave him the consecrated bread, since there was no bread there except the bread of the Presence that had been removed from before the LORD and replaced by hot bread on the day it was taken away.

⁷ Now one of Saul's servants was there that day, detained before the LORD; he was Doeg the Edomite, Saul's chief shepherd.

⁸ David asked Ahimelek, "Don't you have a spear or a sword here? I haven't brought my sword or any other weapon, because the king's mission was urgent."

⁹ The priest replied, "The sword of Goliath the Philistine, whom you killed in the Valley of Elah, is here; it is wrapped in a cloth behind the ephod. If you want it, take it; there is no sword here but that one."

David said, "There is none like it; give it to me."

¹⁰ That day David fled from Saul and went to Achish king of Gath. ¹¹ But the servants of Achish said to him, "Isn't this David, the king of the land? Isn't he the one they sing about in their dances:

"'Saul has slain his thousands,
    and David his tens of thousands'?"

¹² David took these words to heart and was very much afraid of Achish king of Gath. ¹³ So he pretended to be insane in their presence; and while he was in their hands he acted like a madman, making marks on the doors of the gate and letting saliva run down his beard.

¹⁴ Achish said to his servants, "Look at the man! He is insane! Why bring him to me? ¹⁵ Am I so short of madmen that you have to bring this

fellow here to carry on like this in front of me? Must this man come into my house?"

NEW KING JAMES VERSION

^{19:4} Thus Jonathan spoke well of David to Saul his father, and said to him, "Let not the king sin against his servant, against David, because he has not sinned against you, and because his works have been very good toward you. ⁵ For he took his life in his hands and killed the Philistine, and the LORD brought about a great deliverance for all Israel. You saw it and rejoiced. Why then will you sin against innocent blood, to kill David without a cause?"

⁶ So Saul heeded the voice of Jonathan, and Saul swore, "As the LORD lives, he shall not be killed." ⁷ Then Jonathan called David, and Jonathan told him all these things. So Jonathan brought David to Saul, and he was in his presence as in times past.

⁸ And there was war again; and David went out and fought with the Philistines, and struck them with a mighty blow, and they fled from him.

⁹ Now the distressing spirit from the LORD came upon Saul as he sat in his house with his spear in his hand. And David was playing music with his hand. ¹⁰ Then Saul sought to pin David to the wall with the spear, but he slipped away from Saul's presence; and he drove the spear into the wall. So David fled and escaped that night.

^{21:1} Now David came to Nob, to Ahimelech the priest. And Ahimelech was afraid when he met David, and said to him, "Why are you alone, and no one is with you?"

² So David said to Ahimelech the priest, "The king has ordered me on some business, and said to me, 'Do not let anyone know anything about the business on which I send you, or what I have commanded you.' And I have directed my young men to such and such a place. ³ Now therefore, what have you on hand? Give me five loaves of bread in my hand, or whatever can be found."

⁴ And the priest answered David and said, "There is no common bread on hand; but there is holy bread, if the young men have at least kept themselves from women."

⁵ Then David answered the priest, and said to him, "Truly, women have been kept from us about three days since I came out. And the vessels of the young men are holy, and the bread is in effect common, even though it was consecrated in the vessel this day."

⁶ So the priest gave him holy bread; for there was no bread there but the showbread which had been taken from before the LORD, in order to put hot bread in its place on the day when it was taken away.

⁷ Now a certain man of the servants of Saul was there that day, detained before the LORD. And his name was Doeg, an Edomite, the chief of the herdsmen who belonged to Saul.

⁸ And David said to Ahimelech, "Is there not here on hand a spear or a sword? For I have brought neither my sword nor my weapons with me, because the king's business required haste."

⁹ So the priest said, "The sword of Goliath the Philistine, whom you killed in the Valley of Elah, there it is, wrapped in a cloth behind the ephod. If you will take that, take it. For there is no other except that one here."

And David said, "There is none like it; give it to me."

¹⁰ Then David arose and fled that day from before Saul, and went to Achish the king of Gath. ¹¹ And the servants of Achish said to him, "Is this not David the king of the land? Did they not sing of him to one another in dances, saying:

'Saul has slain his thousands,
And David his ten thousands'?"

¹² Now David took these words to heart, and was very much afraid of Achish the king of Gath. ¹³ So he changed his behavior before them, pretended madness in their hands, scratched on the doors of the gate, and let his saliva fall down on his beard. ¹⁴ Then Achish said to his servants,

"Look, you see the man is insane. Why have you brought him to me? ¹⁵ Have I need of madmen, that you have brought this fellow to play the madman in my presence? Shall this fellow come into my house?"

EXPLORATION

1. What did Jonathan say to his father to try and convince him that David had done no wrong against him? How did Jonathan speak up on behalf of David?

_____

_____

_____

_____

2. What promise did Saul make to his son Jonathan? Why do you think David—given that Saul had made numerous attempts on his life—agreed to go back into the king's service?

_____

_____

_____

_____

3. David sought sanctuary from Saul in a priestly town called Nob. How did David respond to Ahimelek, the priest, when asked why he and his men were there?

_____

_____

_____

4. What might have compelled David to lie to Ahimelek? How did David convince the priest to allow him and his men to eat the consecrated bread?

_____

_____

_____

_____

_____

5. How did David explain why he was unarmed? What did the priest offer to give to him?

_____

_____

_____

_____

_____

_____

6. What did the people of Gath recognize when David entered their city? What ruse did David come up with to get Achish, the king of Gath, to release him?

_____

_____

_____

_____

_____

_____

INSPIRATION

David is now on the lam, a wanted man in Saul's court. His young face decorates post office posters. His name tops Saul's to-kill list. He runs, looking over his shoulder, sleeping with one eye open, and eating with his chair next to the restaurant exit.

After the sixth attempt on his life, David gets the point. *Saul doesn't like me.* With a price on his head and a posse on his trail, he kisses Michal and life in the court goodbye and runs. But where can he go? To Bethlehem and jeopardize the lives of his family? Into enemy territory and risk his own? That becomes an option later. For now, he chooses another hideout. He goes to church. "David went to Nob, to Ahimelek the priest" (1 Samuel 21:1).

His arrival stirs understandable fear in Ahimelek. What brings a warrior to Nob? What does the son-in-law of the king want? David buys assurance by lying: "The king sent me on a mission and said to me, 'No one is to know anything about the mission I am sending you on'" (verse 2). Desperate, David resorts to mistruth.

David's faith is clearly wavering. Not too long ago the shepherd's sling was all he needed. Now the one who refused the armor and sword of Saul requests a weapon from the priest. What has happened to our hero? Simple. He's lost his God-focus.

Goliath is on the big screen of David's imagination. As a result, desperation has set in. Lie-spawning, fear-stirring, truth-shading desperation. No place to hide. No food to eat. No recourse. No resource. Where can he go? Where can all those who are desperate—teenaged and pregnant, middle-aged and broke, old-aged and sick—go to find safety?

They can go to God's sanctuary. God's church. They can look for an Ahimelek, a church leader with a heart for desperate souls. To the spiritually hungry, the church offers nourishment: "Neither death nor life, neither angels nor demons, neither the present nor the future, nor any powers, neither height nor depth, nor anything else in all creation, will be able to separate us from the love of God that is in Christ Jesus"

(Romans 8:38–39). To the fugitive, the church offers weapons of truth: "In all things God works for the good of those who love him, who have been called according to his purpose" (verse 28).

Bread and blades. Food and equipment. The church exists to provide both.

Ahimelek teaches the church to pursue the spirit of the law more than its letter. David teaches the desperate to seek help amidst God's people. David stumbles in this story. Desperate souls always do. But at least he stumbles into the right place—into God's sanctuary, where God meets and ministers to hopeless hearts. (From *Facing Your Giants* by Max Lucado.)

REACTION

7. David was now in a desperate situation. How do you think he was feeling at this moment? When have you encountered this kind of desperation in your life?

_____

_____

_____

_____

_____

8. Desperation caused David to lie. When the pressure is mounting and you are feeling desperate, what do you do to make sure you don't compromise your values?

_____

_____

_____

_____

_____

9. What does this story reveal about what happens when you lose your God-focus?

10. How has the church served as a sanctuary for you?

11. Who are some of the "Ahimeleks" in your life . . . those leaders who helped you when you were in need? What did those people do that especially ministered to you?

12. David stumbles in this story, but at least he stumbles into the right place. How have you seen God lift you up when you have stumbled in following him?

_____

_____

_____

_____

_____

_____

_____

LIFE LESSONS

David's actions in this portion of 1 Samuel reveal that even though he was "a man after [God's] own heart," (1 Samuel 13:14), he still followed his own heart at times. So far, David has been portrayed as stellar, spotless, and stainless. He stayed calm when his brothers snapped, remained strong when Goliath roared, and kept his cool when Saul lost his head. But now, we find him lying to a priest of God and then playing loose with Scripture to get bread for his men. The fact that even _David_ could stumble should be an encouragement to us. For even though he faltered, we find him inquiring of the Lord again just a few chapters later—and the Lord responding. We all, like David, stumble along the way. Yet we have the assurance, "If we confess our sins, [God] is faithful and just and will forgive us our sins" (1 John 1:9).

DEVOTION

Lord, we praise you today for your promise to be with us in the desperate days. Forgive us for the times we lose our way and follow after our own hearts rather than your heart. Thank you for your mercy toward us when we do stumble and falter on the path you have set before us.

JOURNALING

Helping David would prove to be costly to both Jonathan and Ahimelek. What might the cost be for you (in terms of time and resources) in helping those going through desperate times?

FOR FURTHER READING

To complete the book of 1 Samuel during this twelve-part study, read 1 Samuel 19:1–21:15. For more Bible passages about God's forgiveness, read Psalm 32:5; 103:12; Proverbs 28:13; Isaiah 1:18; Matthew 6:14–15; Romans 3:23–24; Ephesians 1:7–10; Colossians 1:13–14.

DEALING WITH DRY SEASONS

Saul and his men began the search, and when David was told about it, he went down to the rock and stayed in the Desert of Maon.
1 SAMUEL 23:25

REFLECTION

What was a "dry season" in your life? What made it such a difficult time for you?

_____

_____

_____

_____

_____

_____

_____

_____

_____

_____

_____

_____

SITUATION

Jonathan's attempts to curb his father's anger against David had failed . . . a "point" that was made especially clear when Saul hurled a spear at *him*. David's only choice was to go into hiding with his men. His first stop was Nob, where the priest Ahimelek gave him bread and the sword of Goliath. His next stop was Gath, where he tried to go unnoticed among Israel's enemies, the Philistines. When David was discovered, he feigned madness, was released, and made his way to Moab. Meanwhile, Saul learned that Ahimelek had helped David and ordered eighty-five of the priests be killed and the town of Nob destroyed. Only one survivor, a son of Ahimelek, was able to escape to inform David of the massacre. It was the beginning of a long dry season for David . . . a game of hide-and-seek with Saul where the cost of losing was his very life.

OBSERVATION

*Read 1 Samuel 23:7–29 from the New International
Version or the New King James Version.*

New International Version

⁷ Saul was told that David had gone to Keilah, and he said, "God has delivered him into my hands, for David has imprisoned himself by entering a town with gates and bars." ⁸ And Saul called up all his forces for battle, to go down to Keilah to besiege David and his men.

⁹ When David learned that Saul was plotting against him, he said to Abiathar the priest, "Bring the ephod." ¹⁰ David said, "Lord, God of Israel, your servant has heard definitely that Saul plans to come to Keilah and destroy the town on account of me. ¹¹ Will the citizens of Keilah surrender me to him? Will Saul come down, as your servant has heard? Lord, God of Israel, tell your servant."

And the Lord said, "He will."

¹² Again David asked, "Will the citizens of Keilah surrender me and my men to Saul?"

And the Lord said, "They will."

¹³ So David and his men, about six hundred in number, left Keilah and kept moving from place to place. When Saul was told that David had escaped from Keilah, he did not go there.

¹⁴ David stayed in the wilderness strongholds and in the hills of the Desert of Ziph. Day after day Saul searched for him, but God did not give David into his hands.

¹⁵ While David was at Horesh in the Desert of Ziph, he learned that Saul had come out to take his life. ¹⁶ And Saul's son Jonathan went to David at Horesh and helped him find strength in God. ¹⁷ "Don't be afraid," he said. "My father Saul will not lay a hand on you. You will be king over Israel, and I will be second to you. Even my father Saul knows this." ¹⁸ The two of them made a covenant before the Lord. Then Jonathan went home, but David remained at Horesh.

[19] The Ziphites went up to Saul at Gibeah and said, "Is not David hiding among us in the strongholds at Horesh, on the hill of Hakilah, south of Jeshimon? [20] Now, Your Majesty, come down whenever it pleases you to do so, and we will be responsible for giving him into your hands."

[21] Saul replied, "The LORD bless you for your concern for me. [22] Go and get more information. Find out where David usually goes and who has seen him there. They tell me he is very crafty. [23] Find out about all the hiding places he uses and come back to me with definite information. Then I will go with you; if he is in the area, I will track him down among all the clans of Judah."

[24] So they set out and went to Ziph ahead of Saul. Now David and his men were in the Desert of Maon, in the Arabah south of Jeshimon. [25] Saul and his men began the search, and when David was told about it, he went down to the rock and stayed in the Desert of Maon. When Saul heard this, he went into the Desert of Maon in pursuit of David.

[26] Saul was going along one side of the mountain, and David and his men were on the other side, hurrying to get away from Saul. As Saul and his forces were closing in on David and his men to capture them, [27] a messenger came to Saul, saying, "Come quickly! The Philistines are raiding the land." [28] Then Saul broke off his pursuit of David and went to meet the Philistines. That is why they call this place Sela Hammahlekoth. [29] And David went up from there and lived in the strongholds of En Gedi.

NEW KING JAMES VERSION

[7] And Saul was told that David had gone to Keilah. So Saul said, "God has delivered him into my hand, for he has shut himself in by entering a town that has gates and bars." [8] Then Saul called all the people together for war, to go down to Keilah to besiege David and his men.

[9] When David knew that Saul plotted evil against him, he said to Abiathar the priest, "Bring the ephod here." [10] Then David said, "O LORD God of Israel, Your servant has certainly heard that Saul seeks to come to Keilah to destroy the city for my sake. [11] Will the men of Keilah deliver

me into his hand? Will Saul come down, as Your servant has heard? O Lord God of Israel, I pray, tell Your servant."

And the Lord said, "He will come down."

¹² Then David said, "Will the men of Keilah deliver me and my men into the hand of Saul?"

And the Lord said, "They will deliver you."

¹³ So David and his men, about six hundred, arose and departed from Keilah and went wherever they could go. Then it was told Saul that David had escaped from Keilah; so he halted the expedition.

¹⁴ And David stayed in strongholds in the wilderness, and remained in the mountains in the Wilderness of Ziph. Saul sought him every day, but God did not deliver him into his hand. ¹⁵ So David saw that Saul had come out to seek his life. And David was in the Wilderness of Ziph in a forest. ¹⁶ Then Jonathan, Saul's son, arose and went to David in the woods and strengthened his hand in God. ¹⁷ And he said to him, "Do not fear, for the hand of Saul my father shall not find you. You shall be king over Israel, and I shall be next to you. Even my father Saul knows that." ¹⁸ So the two of them made a covenant before the Lord. And David stayed in the woods, and Jonathan went to his own house.

¹⁹ Then the Ziphites came up to Saul at Gibeah, saying, "Is David not hiding with us in strongholds in the woods, in the hill of Hachilah, which is on the south of Jeshimon? ²⁰ Now therefore, O king, come down according to all the desire of your soul to come down; and our part shall be to deliver him into the king's hand."

²¹ And Saul said, "Blessed are you of the Lord, for you have compassion on me. ²² Please go and find out for sure, and see the place where his hideout is, and who has seen him there. For I am told he is very crafty. ²³ See therefore, and take knowledge of all the lurking places where he hides; and come back to me with certainty, and I will go with you. And it shall be, if he is in the land, that I will search for him throughout all the clans of Judah."

²⁴ So they arose and went to Ziph before Saul. But David and his men were in the Wilderness of Maon, in the plain on the south of Jeshimon.

[25] When Saul and his men went to seek him, they told David. Therefore he went down to the rock, and stayed in the Wilderness of Maon. And when Saul heard that, he pursued David in the Wilderness of Maon. [26] Then Saul went on one side of the mountain, and David and his men on the other side of the mountain. So David made haste to get away from Saul, for Saul and his men were encircling David and his men to take them.

[27] But a messenger came to Saul, saying, "Hurry and come, for the Philistines have invaded the land!" [28] Therefore Saul returned from pursuing David, and went against the Philistines; so they called that place the Rock of Escape. [29] Then David went up from there and dwelt in strongholds at En Gedi.

EXPLORATION

1. What did Saul say when he learned that David had gone to Keilah? Why was he certain that he could capture David in that town?

_____

_____

_____

2. What did the Lord reveal to David about Saul's movements? What did God reveal about what the citizens of Keilah would do once he arrived?

_____

_____

_____

3. What help did Jonathan provide to David when he met him at Horesh? What did Jonathan say the Lord had planned for David's life?

_____

_____

_____

4. What mission did Saul give the Ziphites when they revealed that David was in Horesh?

5. What did David do when he learned that Saul was in Ziph? How was he able to elude a confrontation with Saul's men in the Desert of Maon?

6. What finally compelled Saul to call off the search for David?

INSPIRATION

No one chooses the wilderness. It comes at you from all directions—heat and rain, sandstorms and hail. We prefer air-conditioned bedrooms and cul-de-sac safety. But sometimes we have no vote. Calamity hits and the roof rips. The tornado lifts and drops us in the desert. Not the desert in southeastern Israel, but the desert of the soul. A season of dryness.

Isolation marks such seasons. This is certainly true in David's story. Saul has effectively and systematically isolated him from every source of stability. He can't go to the court of Saul, or the house of Michal, or the city of Samuel, or the safety of Nob. He can do nothing but run.

Wilderness begins with disconnections. It continues with deceit. We saw David's deceit in Nob, the city of the priests. The city was holy; David was anything but. He lied each time he opened his mouth. David gets worse before he gets better. He escapes to Gath, the hometown of Goliath. He tries to forge a friendship based on a mutual adversary. If your enemy is Saul and my enemy is Saul, we become friends, right?

In this case, wrong. The Gittites aren't hospitable.

David pretends to be insane, scratching on doors and drooling down his beard. Finally the king of Gath says to his men, "Must you bring me a madman? We already have enough of them around here! Why should I let someone like this be my guest?" (1 Samuel 21:14–15 NLT). They shove him out the city gates and leave him with nowhere to go.

So David goes to the only place he can—the place where no one goes, because nothing survives. He goes to the desert, the wilderness— to the honeycombed canyons that overlook the Dead Sea. He finds a cave, the cave called Adullam. In it he finds shade, silence, and safety. He stretches out on the cool dirt and closes his eyes and begins his decade in the wilderness.

Can you relate to David? Has your Saul cut you off from the position you had and people you love? In an effort to land on your feet, have you stretched the truth? Distorted the facts? Are you seeking refuge in Gath?

Under normal circumstances you would never go there. But these aren't normal circumstances, so you loiter in the breeding ground of giants. The hometown of trouble. Her arms or that bar. You walk shady streets and frequent questionable places. And, while there, you go crazy. So the crowd will accept you, so the stress won't kill you, you go wild. You wake up in the grottoes of Adullam, at the lowest point of your life, feeling as dumb as a roomful of anvils. You stare out at an arid, harsh, unpeopled future and ask, "What do I do now?"

I suggest you let David be your teacher. Sure, he goes wacko for a few verses. But in the cave of Adullam, he gathers himself. The faithful shepherd boy surfaces again. The giant-killer rediscovers courage. Yes, he has a price on his head. Yes, he has no place to lay his head, but somehow he keeps his head. He returns his focus to God and finds refuge.

Do the same. Make *God* your refuge—not your job, your spouse, your reputation, or your retirement account. Let him, not Saul, encircle you. Let him be the ceiling that breaks the sunshine, the walls that stop the wind, the foundation on which you stand.

Wilderness survivors find refuge in God's presence. They also discover community among God's people. Strong congregations are populated with current and former cave dwellers, people who know the terrain of Adullam. They told a few lies in Nob. They went loopy in Gath. They haven't forgotten it. And because they haven't, they imitate David: They make room for you. Find comfort in his people. Cast your hat in a congregation of folks who are one gift of grace removed from tragedy, addiction, and disaster.

Seek community in the church of Adullam. Refuge in God's presence. Comfort in God's people. These are your keys for wilderness survival. Do this, and, who knows, in the midst of this desert you may write your sweetest psalms. (From *Facing Your Giants* by Max Lucado.)

REACTION

7. David's season of dryness was marked by isolation. When is a time in your life that you felt isolated from others? What effect did that have on your state of mind?

_____

_____

_____

_____

_____

8. David ended up in the city of Gath. What represents "enemy territory" in your life—places where you know God doesn't want you to go?

_____

_____

_____

9. David eventually found peace and safety in the cave of Adullam. What brings you the most peace and security when you are going through difficult seasons?

_____

_____

_____

_____

10. It was in the cave that David wrote, "Have mercy on me, my God . . . for in you I take refuge" (Psalm 57:1). How has God been your refuge?

_____

_____

_____

11. David did not remain isolated in the wilderness: "All those who were in distress or in debt or discontented gathered around him" (1 Samuel 22:2). How do you think this community helped David? How has your community helped you in dry seasons?

_____

_____

_____

_____

12. What are some of the benefits that your seasons of dryness have brought into your life? How did you grow closer to God (and others) after going through those times?

_____

_____

_____

_____

_____

_____

_____

_____

_____

LIFE LESSONS

David was in a dry season. Saul had cut him off from the position he held and the people he loved. In an effort to land on his feet, he had stretched the truth and sought refuge with an enemy. He eventually found himself in a cave in the wilderness. It was there, in his isolation, that he remembered he was *not* alone. David regained his God-focus . . . and penned a few psalms in the process. We need to follow David's example in our wilderness moments. When we feel abandoned and alone, we should remember that God has promised, "Never will I leave you; never will I forsake you" (Hebrews 13:5). He is with us even in the dry seasons.

DEVOTION

Lord God, be our shepherd during the dry seasons in life. Lead us to green pastures and quiet waters where our souls can be refreshed in you. Help us to remember that we are never alone, for you have promised to never leave us, forsake us, or abandon us in the valleys of life.

JOURNALING

David regained his God-focus in the solitude of the wilderness. What does his story reveal about how to get through spiritual dry seasons in your life? What are some ways that you have found to be the most effective in regaining your God-focus when you feel distant from the Lord?

_____

_____

_____

_____

_____

_____

_____

_____

_____

_____

_____

_____

_____

_____

_____

_____

_____

_____

_____

FOR FURTHER READING

To complete the book of 1 Samuel during this twelve-part study, read 1 Samuel 22:1–23:29. For more Bible passages about finding refuge in God, read Psalm 62:8; 91:1–2; Proverbs 18:10; Jeremiah 17:5–7; Matthew 8:26–27; John 10:9; Ephesians 2:4–6; Hebrews 13:6.

THE GOD-SATURATED MIND

"The Lord forbid that I should do such a thing to my master . . . for he is the anointed of the Lord."
1 Samuel 24:6

REFLECTION

What makes it so hard to *not* seek revenge against those people who wrong you?

_____

_____

_____

_____

_____

_____

_____

_____

_____

_____

_____

_____

_____

SITUATION

When Saul learned that David had attacked the Philistines at the Israelite village of Keilah, he thought he had at last cornered his foe, for David had entered "a town with gates and bars" (1 Samuel 23:7). However, David learned of Saul's plans and inquired of the Lord as to whether the people of Keilah would betray him. When God revealed that they would, David took his six hundred men and fled into the Desert of Ziph. The Ziphites learned that he was there and reported his location to Saul, which prompted the king to set out again in search of David. Ultimately, when Saul learned that David was in the Desert of Maon, and in a deadly game of cat-and-mouse, his forces went up one side of a mountain while David and his men went down the other side. A report of a Philistine raid prompted Saul to break off the pursuit, but he soon returned to the chase—leading his men to a place called the Crags of the Wild Goats.

OBSERVATION

Read 1 Samuel 24:1–22 from the New International Version or the New King James Version.

New International Version

¹ After Saul returned from pursuing the Philistines, he was told, "David is in the Desert of En Gedi." ² So Saul took three thousand able young men from all Israel and set out to look for David and his men near the Crags of the Wild Goats.

³ He came to the sheep pens along the way; a cave was there, and Saul went in to relieve himself. David and his men were far back in the cave. ⁴ The men said, "This is the day the Lord spoke of when he said to you, 'I will give your enemy into your hands for you to deal with as you wish.'" Then David crept up unnoticed and cut off a corner of Saul's robe.

⁵ Afterward, David was conscience-stricken for having cut off a corner of his robe. ⁶ He said to his men, "The Lord forbid that I should do such a thing to my master, the Lord's anointed, or lay my hand on him; for he is the anointed of the Lord." ⁷ With these words David sharply rebuked his men and did not allow them to attack Saul. And Saul left the cave and went his way.

⁸ Then David went out of the cave and called out to Saul, "My lord the king!" When Saul looked behind him, David bowed down and prostrated himself with his face to the ground. ⁹ He said to Saul, "Why do you listen when men say, 'David is bent on harming you'? ¹⁰ This day you have seen with your own eyes how the Lord delivered you into my hands in the cave. Some urged me to kill you, but I spared you; I said, 'I will not lay my hand on my lord, because he is the Lord's anointed.' ¹¹ See, my father, look at this piece of your robe in my hand! I cut off the corner of your robe but did not kill you. See that there is nothing in my hand to indicate that I am guilty of wrongdoing or rebellion. I have not wronged you, but you are hunting me down to take my life. ¹² May the Lord judge between you and me. And may the Lord avenge the wrongs you have done to me,

but my hand will not touch you. ¹³ As the old saying goes, 'From evildoers come evil deeds,' so my hand will not touch you.

¹⁴ "Against whom has the king of Israel come out? Who are you pursuing? A dead dog? A flea? ¹⁵ May the Lord be our judge and decide between us. May he consider my cause and uphold it; may he vindicate me by delivering me from your hand."

¹⁶ When David finished saying this, Saul asked, "Is that your voice, David my son?" And he wept aloud. ¹⁷ "You are more righteous than I," he said. "You have treated me well, but I have treated you badly. ¹⁸ You have just now told me about the good you did to me; the LORD delivered me into your hands, but you did not kill me. ¹⁹ When a man finds his enemy, does he let him get away unharmed? May the LORD reward you well for the way you treated me today. ²⁰ I know that you will surely be king and that the kingdom of Israel will be established in your hands. ²¹ Now swear to me by the LORD that you will not kill off my descendants or wipe out my name from my father's family."

²² So David gave his oath to Saul. Then Saul returned home, but David and his men went up to the stronghold.

NEW KING JAMES VERSION

¹ Now it happened, when Saul had returned from following the Philistines, that it was told him, saying, "Take note! David is in the Wilderness of En Gedi." ² Then Saul took three thousand chosen men from all Israel, and went to seek David and his men on the Rocks of the Wild Goats. ³ So he came to the sheepfolds by the road, where there was a cave; and Saul went in to attend to his needs. (David and his men were staying in the recesses of the cave.) ⁴ Then the men of David said to him, "This is the day of which the LORD said to you, 'Behold, I will deliver your enemy into your hand, that you may do to him as it seems good to you.'" And David arose and secretly cut off a corner of Saul's robe. ⁵ Now it happened afterward that David's heart troubled him because he had cut Saul's robe. ⁶ And he said to his men, "The LORD forbid that I should do this thing to my master, the LORD's anointed, to stretch out my hand against him, seeing he is

the anointed of the LORD." ⁷ So David restrained his servants with these words, and did not allow them to rise against Saul. And Saul got up from the cave and went on his way.

⁸ David also arose afterward, went out of the cave, and called out to Saul, saying, "My lord the king!" And when Saul looked behind him, David stooped with his face to the earth, and bowed down. ⁹ And David said to Saul: "Why do you listen to the words of men who say, 'Indeed David seeks your harm'? ¹⁰ Look, this day your eyes have seen that the LORD delivered you today into my hand in the cave, and someone urged me to kill you. But my eye spared you, and I said, 'I will not stretch out my hand against my lord, for he is the LORD's anointed.' ¹¹ Moreover, my father, see! Yes, see the corner of your robe in my hand! For in that I cut off the corner of your robe, and did not kill you, know and see that there is neither evil nor rebellion in my hand, and I have not sinned against you. Yet you hunt my life to take it. ¹² Let the LORD judge between you and me, and let the LORD avenge me on you. But my hand shall not be against you. ¹³ As the proverb of the ancients says, 'Wickedness proceeds from the wicked.' But my hand shall not be against you. ¹⁴ After whom has the king of Israel come out? Whom do you pursue? A dead dog? A flea? ¹⁵ Therefore let the LORD be judge, and judge between you and me, and see and plead my case, and deliver me out of your hand."

¹⁶ So it was, when David had finished speaking these words to Saul, that Saul said, "Is this your voice, my son David?" And Saul lifted up his voice and wept. ¹⁷ Then he said to David: "You are more righteous than I; for you have rewarded me with good, whereas I have rewarded you with evil. ¹⁸ And you have shown this day how you have dealt well with me; for when the LORD delivered me into your hand, you did not kill me. ¹⁹ For if a man finds his enemy, will he let him get away safely? Therefore may the LORD reward you with good for what you have done to me this day. ²⁰ And now I know indeed that you shall surely be king, and that the kingdom of Israel shall be established in your hand. ²¹ Therefore swear now to me by the LORD that you will not cut off my descendants after me, and that you will not destroy my name from my father's house."

²² So David swore to Saul. And Saul went home, but David and his men went up to the stronghold.

EXPLORATION

1. What did David's men say when they discovered that King Saul had wandered into the cave they were occupying and was completely unaware of their presence?

_____

_____

_____

_____

_____

2. What action did David take in this matter? How did he feel about this immediately after doing it?

_____

_____

_____

_____

_____

_____

3. What reason did David give to his men as to why they could not kill King Saul?

_____

_____

_____

_____

_____

4. How did David prove to Saul that he had spared his life? What did he promise to Saul after saying "from evildoers come evil deeds" (verse 13)?

5. How did Saul react when he realized that David had indeed spared his life? What did Saul admit that he knew about David when it came to God's plans for Israel?

6. What oath did Saul ask David to swear to him before the Lord?

INSPIRATION

David, still on the run, dashes into the desert, where he finds refuge among the caves near the Dead Sea. Several hundred loyalists follow him. So does Saul. And in a dramatic desert scene, David models how to give grace to the person who gives nothing but grief.

Picture the scene. Saul signals for his men to stop. They do. Three thousand soldiers cease their marching as their king dismounts and walks up the mountainside. The region of En Gedi simmers in the brick-oven heat. Sunrays strike daggerlike on the soldiers' necks. Lizards lie behind rocks. Scorpions linger in the dirt. And snakes, like Saul, seek rest in the cave.

Saul enters the cave "to relieve himself." Meanwhile, "David and his men were far back in the cave" (1 Samuel 24:3). With eyes dulled from the desert sun, the king fails to notice the silent figures who line the walls. As Saul heeds nature's call, dozens of eyes widen. Their minds race, and hands reach for daggers. One thrust of the blade will bring Saul's tyranny to an end.

But David signals for his men to hold back. He edges along the wall, unsheathes his knife, and cuts not the flesh but the robe of Saul. David then creeps back into the recesses of the cave. The men can't believe what their leader has done.

Saul exits the cave, and David soon follows. He lifts the garment corner and, in so many words, shouts, "I could have killed you, but I didn't." Saul looks up, stunned, and wonders aloud, "If a man finds his enemy, will he let him get away safely?" (verse 19 NKJV).

David will. More than once.

David faced Saul the way he faced Goliath—by facing God more so. When the soldiers in the cave urged David to kill Saul, look who occupied David's thoughts: "The LORD forbid that I should do such a thing to my master, the LORD's anointed, or lay my hand on him; for he is the anointed of the LORD" (verse 6).

David saw not Saul the *enemy* but Saul the *anointed*. He refused to see his grief-giver as anything less than a child of God. He filtered his view of Saul through the grid of heaven. The king still belonged to God, and that gave David hope.

Notice what David *didn't* do. He didn't applaud Saul's behavior. He didn't gloss over or sidestep Saul's sin. He didn't avoid the issue. But he did avoid Saul. "Saul returned home, but David and his men went up to the stronghold" (verse 22).

Do the same. Give grace to your grief-giver, but, if need be, keep your distance.

Forgiveness is not excusing. It is not pretending. It is not foolishness. Forgiveness, at its core, is simply choosing to see your offender with different eyes. (From *Facing Your Giants* by Max Lucado.)

REACTION

7. David's men were shocked that he did not take revenge against Saul. When has another person's act of grace (maybe toward you) caught you off guard? What happened in that situation?

8. David refused to kill Saul because he was the Lord's anointed. How do you think David was able to view Saul this way after all that Saul had done to him?

9. What would it take for you to see your "Saul" as a child of God?

10. Jesus said, "Love your enemies and pray for those who persecute you" (Matthew 5:44). What are some of the benefits that forgiving your "enemies" has brought to you?

11. David extended grace toward Saul but did not excuse the wrong Saul had done. What does this say about what forgiveness *is* and *is not*?

_____

_____

_____

_____

12. What do you learn from this story about the importance of not seeking vengeance against those who have wronged you?

_____

_____

_____

_____

LIFE LESSONS

David understood an important principle that God had revealed to Moses: "It is mine to avenge; I will repay" (Deuteronomy 32:35). Paul would later reiterate the principle to followers of Christ: "Do not take revenge, my dear friends, but leave room for God's wrath, for it is written: 'It is mine to avenge; I will repay,' says the Lord" (Romans 12:19). The Lord asks us not to extend retribution toward those who have wronged us but *forgiveness*. If David had chosen to kill Saul in the cave, his act of revenge would have removed God from the equation. Instead, he acknowledged that God was sovereign and would deal with Saul in his own way and time.

DEVOTION

Heavenly Father, we confess that it is so easy for us to lash out at others and take revenge! We need your grace to respond in the way that you have called us to respond. Help us to remember the sacrifice that Jesus made for us on the cross and extend forgiveness to everyone.

JOURNALING

Paul wrote, "Forgive each other just as God forgave you in Christ" (Ephesians 4:32 NCV). Forgiving others becomes easier when you remember how God has forgiven you. So do that right now. How will you express your thankfulness to God today for the ways in which he has forgiven you? How has his grace and mercy transformed your life?

FOR FURTHER READING

To complete the book of 1 Samuel during this twelve-part study, read 1 Samuel 24:1–22. For more Bible passages about being merciful to others, read Leviticus 19:18; Proverbs 20:22; Proverbs 31:8–9; Matthew 5:7; James 2:13; Luke 6:36; John 15:12–14; and Jude 1:22–23.

A WELL-SPOKEN WORD

*"Pardon your servant, my lord, and let me speak
to you; hear what your servant has to say."*

1 SAMUEL 25:24

REFLECTION

What strategies do you find most effective for defusing a tense situation?

_____

_____

_____

_____

_____

_____

_____

_____

_____

_____

_____

_____

SITUATION

It seemed the Lord had delivered Saul into David's hands. The men with David certainly believed this to be true, telling their leader, "This is the day the LORD spoke of when he said to you, 'I will give your enemy into your hands for you to deal with as you wish'" (1 Samuel 24:4). It had happened when Saul went to "relieve himself" in the cave where David and his men were hiding. All they had to do was sneak up behind him and cut his life short. Instead, David snuck up behind him and cut off a corner of Saul's robe. He refused to do any harm to Saul because he was intent on respecting the one the Lord had anointed as king. Saul was so moved by the gesture that he returned home—only to pick up the chase again on another day. In the meantime, David went to the Desert of Paran, where he encountered a very unpleasant man.

OBSERVATION

*Read 1 Samuel 25:1–35 from the New International
Version or the New King James Version.*

NEW INTERNATIONAL VERSION

[1] Now Samuel died, and all Israel assembled and mourned for him; and they buried him at his home in Ramah. Then David moved down into the Desert of Paran.

[2] A certain man in Maon, who had property there at Carmel, was very wealthy. He had a thousand goats and three thousand sheep, which he was shearing in Carmel. [3] His name was Nabal and his wife's name was Abigail. She was an intelligent and beautiful woman, but her husband was surly and mean in his dealings—he was a Calebite.

[4] While David was in the wilderness, he heard that Nabal was shearing sheep. [5] So he sent ten young men and said to them, "Go up to Nabal at Carmel and greet him in my name. [6] Say to him: 'Long life to you! Good health to you and your household! And good health to all that is yours!

[7] "'Now I hear that it is sheep-shearing time. When your shepherds were with us, we did not mistreat them, and the whole time they were at Carmel nothing of theirs was missing. [8] Ask your own servants and they will tell you. Therefore be favorable toward my men, since we come at a festive time. Please give your servants and your son David whatever you can find for them.'"

[9] When David's men arrived, they gave Nabal this message in David's name. Then they waited.

[10] Nabal answered David's servants, "Who is this David? Who is this son of Jesse? Many servants are breaking away from their masters these days. [11] Why should I take my bread and water, and the meat I have slaughtered for my shearers, and give it to men coming from who knows where?"

[12] David's men turned around and went back. When they arrived, they reported every word. [13] David said to his men, "Each of you strap

on your sword!" So they did, and David strapped his on as well. About four hundred men went up with David, while two hundred stayed with the supplies.

¹⁴ One of the servants told Abigail, Nabal's wife, "David sent messengers from the wilderness to give our master his greetings, but he hurled insults at them. ¹⁵ Yet these men were very good to us. They did not mistreat us, and the whole time we were out in the fields near them nothing was missing. ¹⁶ Night and day they were a wall around us the whole time we were herding our sheep near them. ¹⁷ Now think it over and see what you can do, because disaster is hanging over our master and his whole household. He is such a wicked man that no one can talk to him."

¹⁸ Abigail acted quickly. She took two hundred loaves of bread, two skins of wine, five dressed sheep, five seahs of roasted grain, a hundred cakes of raisins and two hundred cakes of pressed figs, and loaded them on donkeys. ¹⁹ Then she told her servants, "Go on ahead; I'll follow you." But she did not tell her husband Nabal.

²⁰ As she came riding her donkey into a mountain ravine, there were David and his men descending toward her, and she met them. ²¹ David had just said, "It's been useless—all my watching over this fellow's property in the wilderness so that nothing of his was missing. He has paid me back evil for good. ²² May God deal with David, be it ever so severely, if by morning I leave alive one male of all who belong to him!"

²³ When Abigail saw David, she quickly got off her donkey and bowed down before David with her face to the ground. ²⁴ She fell at his feet and said: "Pardon your servant, my lord, and let me speak to you; hear what your servant has to say. ²⁵ Please pay no attention, my lord, to that wicked man Nabal. He is just like his name—his name means Fool, and folly goes with him. And as for me, your servant, I did not see the men my lord sent. ²⁶ And now, my lord, as surely as the LORD your God lives and as you live, since the LORD has kept you from bloodshed and from avenging yourself with your own hands, may your enemies and all who are intent on harming my lord be like Nabal. ²⁷ And let this gift, which your servant has brought to my lord, be given to the men who follow you.

[28] "Please forgive your servant's presumption. The LORD your God will certainly make a lasting dynasty for my lord, because you fight the LORD's battles, and no wrongdoing will be found in you as long as you live. [29] Even though someone is pursuing you to take your life, the life of my lord will be bound securely in the bundle of the living by the LORD your God, but the lives of your enemies he will hurl away as from the pocket of a sling. [30] When the LORD has fulfilled for my lord every good thing he promised concerning him and has appointed him ruler over Israel, [31] my lord will not have on his conscience the staggering burden of needless bloodshed or of having avenged himself. And when the LORD your God has brought my lord success, remember your servant."

[32] David said to Abigail, "Praise be to the LORD, the God of Israel, who has sent you today to meet me. [33] May you be blessed for your good judgment and for keeping me from bloodshed this day and from avenging myself with my own hands. [34] Otherwise, as surely as the LORD, the God of Israel, lives, who has kept me from harming you, if you had not come quickly to meet me, not one male belonging to Nabal would have been left alive by daybreak."

[35] Then David accepted from her hand what she had brought him and said, "Go home in peace. I have heard your words and granted your request."

New King James Version

[1] Then Samuel died; and the Israelites gathered together and lamented for him, and buried him at his home in Ramah. And David arose and went down to the Wilderness of Paran.

[2] Now there was a man in Maon whose business was in Carmel, and the man was very rich. He had three thousand sheep and a thousand goats. And he was shearing his sheep in Carmel. [3] The name of the man was Nabal, and the name of his wife Abigail. And she was a woman of good understanding and beautiful appearance; but the man was harsh and evil in his doings. He was of the house of Caleb.

[4] When David heard in the wilderness that Nabal was shearing his sheep, [5] David sent ten young men; and David said to the young men, "Go up to Carmel, go to Nabal, and greet him in my name. [6] And thus you shall say to him who lives in prosperity: 'Peace be to you, peace to your house, and peace to all that you have! [7] Now I have heard that you have shearers. Your shepherds were with us, and we did not hurt them, nor was there anything missing from them all the while they were in Carmel. [8] Ask your young men, and they will tell you. Therefore let my young men find favor in your eyes, for we come on a feast day. Please give whatever comes to your hand to your servants and to your son David.' "

[9] So when David's young men came, they spoke to Nabal according to all these words in the name of David, and waited.

[10] Then Nabal answered David's servants, and said, "Who is David, and who is the son of Jesse? There are many servants nowadays who break away each one from his master. [11] Shall I then take my bread and my water and my meat that I have killed for my shearers, and give it to men when I do not know where they are from?"

[12] So David's young men turned on their heels and went back; and they came and told him all these words. [13] Then David said to his men, "Every man gird on his sword." So every man girded on his sword, and David also girded on his sword. And about four hundred men went with David, and two hundred stayed with the supplies.

[14] Now one of the young men told Abigail, Nabal's wife, saying, "Look, David sent messengers from the wilderness to greet our master; and he reviled them. [15] But the men were very good to us, and we were not hurt, nor did we miss anything as long as we accompanied them, when we were in the fields. [16] They were a wall to us both by night and day, all the time we were with them keeping the sheep. [17] Now therefore, know and consider what you will do, for harm is determined against our master and against all his household. For he is such a scoundrel that one cannot speak to him."

[18] Then Abigail made haste and took two hundred loaves of bread, two skins of wine, five sheep already dressed, five seahs of roasted grain,

one hundred clusters of raisins, and two hundred cakes of figs, and loaded them on donkeys. ¹⁹ And she said to her servants, "Go on before me; see, I am coming after you." But she did not tell her husband Nabal.

²⁰ So it was, as she rode on the donkey, that she went down under cover of the hill; and there were David and his men, coming down toward her, and she met them. ²¹ Now David had said, "Surely in vain I have protected all that this fellow has in the wilderness, so that nothing was missed of all that belongs to him. And he has repaid me evil for good. ²² May God do so, and more also, to the enemies of David, if I leave one male of all who belong to him by morning light."

²³ Now when Abigail saw David, she dismounted quickly from the donkey, fell on her face before David, and bowed down to the ground. ²⁴ So she fell at his feet and said: "On me, my lord, on me let this iniquity be! And please let your maidservant speak in your ears, and hear the words of your maidservant. ²⁵ Please, let not my lord regard this scoundrel Nabal. For as his name is, so is he: Nabal is his name, and folly is with him! But I, your maidservant, did not see the young men of my lord whom you sent. ²⁶ Now therefore, my lord, as the LORD lives and as your soul lives, since the LORD has held you back from coming to bloodshed and from avenging yourself with your own hand, now then, let your enemies and those who seek harm for my lord be as Nabal. ²⁷ And now this present which your maidservant has brought to my lord, let it be given to the young men who follow my lord. ²⁸ Please forgive the trespass of your maidservant. For the LORD will certainly make for my lord an enduring house, because my lord fights the battles of the LORD, and evil is not found in you throughout your days. ²⁹ Yet a man has risen to pursue you and seek your life, but the life of my lord shall be bound in the bundle of the living with the LORD your God; and the lives of your enemies He shall sling out, as from the pocket of a sling. ³⁰ And it shall come to pass, when the LORD has done for my lord according to all the good that He has spoken concerning you, and has appointed you ruler over Israel, ³¹ that this will be no grief to you, nor offense of heart to my lord, either that you have shed blood without cause, or that my lord has avenged

himself. But when the LORD has dealt well with my lord, then remember your maidservant."

³² Then David said to Abigail: "Blessed is the LORD God of Israel, who sent you this day to meet me! ³³ And blessed is your advice and blessed are you, because you have kept me this day from coming to bloodshed and from avenging myself with my own hand. ³⁴ For indeed, as the LORD God of Israel lives, who has kept me back from hurting you, unless you had hurried and come to meet me, surely by morning light no males would have been left to Nabal!" ³⁵ So David received from her hand what she had brought him, and said to her, "Go up in peace to your house. See, I have heeded your voice and respected your person."

EXPLORATION

1. How is Nabal described in verses 2–3? How is Abigail described?

_____

_____

_____

_____

2. What request did David make of Nabal concerning his men? Why did David believe that Nabal should feel compelled to honor his request?

_____

_____

_____

3. How did Nabal respond to David's men when they delivered the request? Why do you think this response prompted outrage in David?

_____

_____

_____

4. What did Abigail immediately do when she learned that Nabal had angered David? What "oath" was David making to himself when Abigail found him in a ravine?

_____

_____

_____

_____

5. Abigail bowed down before David—with her face to the ground—as a sign of respect. How did she convince David to not take action against Nabal and her household?

_____

_____

_____

_____

6. What was David's reaction when he heard Abigail's well-spoken words and saw the gifts that she had brought? What did he say she should be blessed for doing?

_____

_____

_____

_____

_____

INSPIRATION

Selfishness, hatred, and pride. The code of the jungle is alive and well today. _It's everyone for themselves. Get all you can, and can all you get. Survival of the fittest._

Does the code contaminate your world? Do personal possessive pronouns dominate the language of your circle? *My* career, *my* dreams, *my* stuff. I want things to go *my* way on *my* schedule. If so, you know how savage this giant can be. Yet, every so often, a diamond glitters in the mud. A comrade shares, a soldier cares, or Abigail, stunning Abigail, stands on your trail.

She lived in the days of David and was married to Nabal, whose name means "fool" in Hebrew. He lived up to the definition. "[Nabal] was surly and mean in his dealings . . . such a wicked man that no one [could] talk to him" (1 Samuel 25:3, 17). He never met a person he couldn't anger or a relationship he couldn't spoil. Nabal's world revolved around one person—Nabal. He owed nothing to anybody and laughed at the thought of sharing with anyone.

Nabal and David inhabited the territory—and did so with the harmony of two bulls in the same pasture. It was just a matter of time before they collided. Trouble began to brew after the harvest. With sheep sheared and hay gathered, it was time to bake bread, roast lamb, and pour wine. Take a break from the furrows and flocks and enjoy the fruit of the labor.

As we pick up the story, Nabal's men are doing just that. David hears of the gala and thinks his men deserve an invitation. After all, they've protected Nabal's crops and sheep, patrolled the hills, and secured the valleys. But boorish Nabal scoffs at the thought and pretends he's never heard of David, lumping him in with runaway slaves and vagabonds.

Such insolence infuriates David. He tells the men to form a posse. Or, more precisely, "Strap on your swords!" (verse 12 MSG). Four hundred men mount up and take off. Eyes glare. Nostrils flare. Lips snarl. Testosterone flows. David and his troops thunder down on Nabal. The road rumbles as David grumbles, "May God do his worst to me if Nabal and every cur in his misbegotten brood aren't dead meat by morning!" (verse 22 MSG).

Then, all of a sudden, beauty appears. A daisy lifts her head in the desert. Abigail, the wife of Nabal, stands on the trail. She knows the importance of the moment. She stands as the final barrier between her family and sure death. Falling at David's feet, she issues a plea worthy of a paragraph in Scripture: "Pardon your servant, my lord, and let me speak to you; hear what your servant has to say" (verse 24).

Abigail begs not for justice but forgiveness, accepting blame when she deserves none. "Please forgive your servant's presumption" (verse 28). She offers the gifts from her house and urges David to leave Nabal to God and avoid the dead weight of remorse. Her words fall on David like July sun on ice. He melts. He returns to camp. Abigail returns to Nabal.

Abigail's gentleness reversed a river of anger. Humility has such power. Apologies can disarm arguments. Contrition can defuse rage. Olive branches do more good than battle-axes ever will. "Soft speech can crush strong opposition" (Proverbs 25:15 NLT).

Her example teaches us so much. The contagious power of kindness. The strength of a gentle heart. Her greatest lesson, however, is to take our eyes from her beauty and set them on someone else's. She lifts our thoughts from a rural trail to a Jerusalem cross.

Do you find your Nabal hard to stomach? Then stop staring at him and shift your gaze to Christ. "Don't let evil get the best of you; get the best of evil by doing good" (Romans 12:21 MSG). One Abigail can save a family. Your words can be the beauty amidst your beasts. (From *Facing Your Giants* by Max Lucado.)

REACTION

7. The "code of the jungle" says *it's everyone for themselves . . . get all you can as soon as you can.* How is this code alive and well in society today?

---

8. Nabal dismissed the protection that David's men had offered to his servants and flocks. When is a time you felt your good deeds were being overlooked by another person?

9. How do you typically react when you feel slighted by others?

10. Why is it so hard do what Abigail did in this story? What power do you see in her words?

11. Abigail teaches us the contagious power of kindness and the strength of a gentle heart. How have you seen the power of kindness transform a situation or a person's life?

12. How can you be an "Abigail" to the people in your world today?

_____

_____

_____

_____

_____

_____

_____

_____

_____

_____

LIFE LESSONS

"The words of the reckless pierce like swords, but the tongue of the wise brings healing" (Proverbs 12:18). Nabal was the epitome of a person whose words pierced like swords. He not only refused to recognize the protection that David was providing but also called David's character into question, saying, "Many servants are breaking away from their masters these days" (1 Samuel 25:10). His piercing words prompted David to return the favor with a few sword pierces of his own. But then David met Abigail . . . the epitome of the wise person whose words brings healing. After their encounter, David said, "Go home in peace. I have heard your words and granted your request" (verse 35). God blesses those who bring peace. As Jesus said, "Blessed are the peacemakers, for they will be called children of God" (Matthew 5:9).

DEVOTION

Lord, so often we lash out in anger when we feel slighted by others. Teach us how to be peacemakers . . . just like Abigail was in her dealings with David. As your representatives on this earth, we want to bring calm into the stressful situations we encounter instead of chaos.

JOURNALING

Paul wrote that you "have been sent to speak for Christ" (2 Corinthians 5:20 NCV). How are you using your words to speak on behalf of Christ? What, if anything, needs to change when it comes to the way you interact with others—especially those difficult people in your life?

_____

_____

_____

_____

_____

_____

_____

_____

_____

_____

_____

_____

_____

_____

_____

_____

_____

_____

FOR FURTHER READING

To complete the book of 1 Samuel during this twelve-part study, read 1 Samuel 25:1–28:25. For more Bible passages about guarding your speech, read Psalm 39:1; 141:3; Proverbs 17:27; Ephesians 4:29; Colossians 4:6; Titus 3:1–2; James 3:5–6; 1 Peter 4:11.

IT'S OKAY TO REST

Two hundred of them were too exhausted to cross the valley,
but David and the other four hundred continued the pursuit.
1 Samuel 30:10

REFLECTION

Do you give yourself "permission" to rest—or do you feel you need to always be on the go? What might the cost be to your health and your relationships if you never slow down?

_____

_____

_____

_____

_____

_____

_____

_____

_____

_____

_____

SITUATION

Abigail's well-spoken words had assuaged David's anger toward Nabal. However, ten days later, "the LORD struck Nabal and he died" (1 Samuel 25:38). David, upon hearing the news, asked Abigail to become his wife. Following this, the Ziphites informed Saul that David was back in the region, and Saul set out once more to end his rival's life. This led to a second opportunity for David to kill Saul, but once again he refused, only taking Saul's spear and water jug. In a repeat performance, Saul was moved by David's act and returned home. After this, David returned to the land of the Philistines, where Achish, the Philistine king, agreed to let David, his men, and their families live in the town of Ziklag in exchange for fighting on their side. Sometime later, the Philistines gathered to attack Israel. Saul, in terror, consulted a witch for guidance. Meanwhile,

David marched out with the Philistines to attack Israel—but command-ers refused to go into battle with him, and so David was sent back to Ziklag. It took David and his men three days to reach the town . . . and they were shocked to find what had happened in their absence.

OBSERVATION

Read 1 Samuel 30:3–25 and 1 Samuel 31:1–6 from the
New International Version or the New King James Version.

NEW INTERNATIONAL VERSION

30:3 When David and his men reached Ziklag, they found it destroyed by fire and their wives and sons and daughters taken captive. 4 So David and his men wept aloud until they had no strength left to weep. 5 David's two wives had been captured—Ahinoam of Jezreel and Abigail, the widow of Nabal of Carmel. 6 David was greatly distressed because the men were talking of stoning him; each one was bitter in spirit because of his sons and daughters. But David found strength in the LORD his God.

7 Then David said to Abiathar the priest, the son of Ahimelek, "Bring me the ephod." Abiathar brought it to him, 8 and David inquired of the LORD, "Shall I pursue this raiding party? Will I overtake them?"

"Pursue them," he answered. "You will certainly overtake them and succeed in the rescue."

9 David and the six hundred men with him came to the Besor Valley, where some stayed behind. 10 Two hundred of them were too exhausted to cross the valley, but David and the other four hundred continued the pursuit.

11 They found an Egyptian in a field and brought him to David. They gave him water to drink and food to eat— 12 part of a cake of pressed figs and two cakes of raisins. He ate and was revived, for he had not eaten any food or drunk any water for three days and three nights.

13 David asked him, "Who do you belong to? Where do you come from?"

He said, "I am an Egyptian, the slave of an Amalekite. My master abandoned me when I became ill three days ago. [14] We raided the Negev of the Kerethites, some territory belonging to Judah and the Negev of Caleb. And we burned Ziklag."

[15] David asked him, "Can you lead me down to this raiding party?"

He answered, "Swear to me before God that you will not kill me or hand me over to my master, and I will take you down to them."

[16] He led David down, and there they were, scattered over the countryside, eating, drinking and reveling because of the great amount of plunder they had taken from the land of the Philistines and from Judah. [17] David fought them from dusk until the evening of the next day, and none of them got away, except four hundred young men who rode off on camels and fled. [18] David recovered everything the Amalekites had taken, including his two wives. [19] Nothing was missing: young or old, boy or girl, plunder or anything else they had taken. David brought everything back. [20] He took all the flocks and herds, and his men drove them ahead of the other livestock, saying, "This is David's plunder."

[21] Then David came to the two hundred men who had been too exhausted to follow him and who were left behind at the Besor Valley. They came out to meet David and the men with him. As David and his men approached, he asked them how they were. [22] But all the evil men and troublemakers among David's followers said, "Because they did not go out with us, we will not share with them the plunder we recovered. However, each man may take his wife and children and go."

[23] David replied, "No, my brothers, you must not do that with what the LORD has given us. He has protected us and delivered into our hands the raiding party that came against us. [24] Who will listen to what you say? The share of the man who stayed with the supplies is to be the same as that of him who went down to the battle. All will share alike." [25] David made this a statute and ordinance for Israel from that day to this.

[31:1] Now the Philistines fought against Israel; the Israelites fled before them, and many fell dead on Mount Gilboa. [2] The Philistines were in hot pursuit of Saul and his sons, and they killed his sons Jonathan, Abinadab and Malki-Shua. ³ The fighting grew fierce around Saul, and when the archers overtook him, they wounded him critically.

⁴ Saul said to his armor-bearer, "Draw your sword and run me through, or these uncircumcised fellows will come and run me through and abuse me."

But his armor-bearer was terrified and would not do it; so Saul took his own sword and fell on it. ⁵ When the armor-bearer saw that Saul was dead, he too fell on his sword and died with him. ⁶ So Saul and his three sons and his armor-bearer and all his men died together that same day.

NEW KING JAMES VERSION

³ So David and his men came to the city, and there it was, burned with fire; and their wives, their sons, and their daughters had been taken captive. ⁴ Then David and the people who were with him lifted up their voices and wept, until they had no more power to weep. ⁵ And David's two wives, Ahinoam the Jezreelitess, and Abigail the widow of Nabal the Carmelite, had been taken captive. ⁶ Now David was greatly distressed, for the people spoke of stoning him, because the soul of all the people was grieved, every man for his sons and his daughters. But David strengthened himself in the LORD his God.

⁷ Then David said to Abiathar the priest, Ahimelech's son, "Please bring the ephod here to me." And Abiathar brought the ephod to David. ⁸ So David inquired of the LORD, saying, "Shall I pursue this troop? Shall I overtake them?"

And He answered him, "Pursue, for you shall surely overtake them and without fail recover all."

⁹ So David went, he and the six hundred men who were with him, and came to the Brook Besor, where those stayed who were left behind. ¹⁰ But David pursued, he and four hundred men; for two hundred stayed behind, who were so weary that they could not cross the Brook Besor.

¹¹ Then they found an Egyptian in the field, and brought him to David; and they gave him bread and he ate, and they let him drink water.

[12] And they gave him a piece of a cake of figs and two clusters of raisins. So when he had eaten, his strength came back to him; for he had eaten no bread nor drunk water for three days and three nights. [13] Then David said to him, "To whom do you belong, and where are you from?"

And he said, "I am a young man from Egypt, servant of an Amalekite; and my master left me behind, because three days ago I fell sick. [14] We made an invasion of the southern area of the Cherethites, in the territory which belongs to Judah, and of the southern area of Caleb; and we burned Ziklag with fire."

[15] And David said to him, "Can you take me down to this troop?"

So he said, "Swear to me by God that you will neither kill me nor deliver me into the hands of my master, and I will take you down to this troop."

[16] And when he had brought him down, there they were, spread out over all the land, eating and drinking and dancing, because of all the great spoil which they had taken from the land of the Philistines and from the land of Judah. [17] Then David attacked them from twilight until the evening of the next day. Not a man of them escaped, except four hundred young men who rode on camels and fled. [18] So David recovered all that the Amalekites had carried away, and David rescued his two wives. [19] And nothing of theirs was lacking, either small or great, sons or daughters, spoil or anything which they had taken from them; David recovered all. [20] Then David took all the flocks and herds they had driven before those other livestock, and said, "This is David's spoil."

[21] Now David came to the two hundred men who had been so weary that they could not follow David, whom they also had made to stay at the Brook Besor. So they went out to meet David and to meet the people who were with him. And when David came near the people, he greeted them. [22] Then all the wicked and worthless men of those who went with David answered and said, "Because they did not go with us, we will not give them any of the spoil that we have recovered, except for every man's wife and children, that they may lead them away and depart."

[23] But David said, "My brethren, you shall not do so with what the LORD has given us, who has preserved us and delivered into our hand the

troop that came against us. ²⁴ For who will heed you in this matter? But as his part is who goes down to the battle, so shall his part be who stays by the supplies; they shall share alike." ²⁵ So it was, from that day forward; he made it a statute and an ordinance for Israel to this day.

³¹:¹ Now the Philistines fought against Israel; and the men of Israel fled from before the Philistines, and fell slain on Mount Gilboa. ² Then the Philistines followed hard after Saul and his sons. And the Philistines killed Jonathan, Abinadab, and Malchishua, Saul's sons. ³ The battle became fierce against Saul. The archers hit him, and he was severely wounded by the archers.

⁴ Then Saul said to his armorbearer, "Draw your sword, and thrust me through with it, lest these uncircumcised men come and thrust me through and abuse me."

But his armorbearer would not, for he was greatly afraid. Therefore Saul took a sword and fell on it. ⁵ And when his armorbearer saw that Saul was dead, he also fell on his sword, and died with him. ⁶ So Saul, his three sons, his armorbearer, and all his men died together that same day.

EXPLORATION

1. David's men were met with a devastating scene when they returned to Ziklag. How did they respond when they discovered their wives and children had been captured?

2. David was "greatly distressed" when he saw his men's bitterness toward him but "found strength in the LORD his God" (30:6). What did God instruct him to do?

_____

_____

_____

_____

_____

_____

3. Why did one-third of David's army give up their pursuit when they arrived in the Besor Valley? What did David and his remaining men find when they continued on?

_____

_____

_____

_____

_____

_____

4. The man whom David's men found in the field was an Egyptian "slave of an Amalekite" (verse 13). What was he ultimately willing to do for David?

_____

_____

_____

_____

_____

_____

_____

5. David and his four hundred men defeated the Amalekites and returned to the other two hundred men who had stayed behind in the Besor Valley. What complaint did some of the four hundred men make at this point? How did David resolve the dispute?

---

6. Samuel had said to Saul, "You have rejected the word of the LORD, and the LORD has rejected you as king over Israel" (1 Samuel 15:26). How did this prophecy come to pass in the final chapter of 1 Samuel?

INSPIRATION

Have you ever reached your "plopping point"? Blame it on your boss. "We need you to take *one more* case." Your spouse. "I'll be out late *one more* night this week." Your parents. "I have *one more* chore for you to do." Your friend. "I need just *one more* favor." The problem? You've handled, tolerated, done, forgiven, and taken until you don't have one more "one more" in you.

David's men had come to this point. The story emerges from the ruins of Ziklag. They returned from the Philistine war front to find utter devastation. A raiding band of Amalekites had swept down on the village, looted it, and taken the women and children hostage.

The sorrow of the men mutates into anger, not against the Amalekites, but against David. After all, hadn't he led them into battle? Hadn't he left the women and children unprotected? Isn't he to blame? Then he needs to die. So they start grabbing stones.

This could have been David's worst hour. But he makes it one of his best. While six hundred men stoke their anger, David seeks his God. "David found strength in the LORD his God" (1 Samuel 30:6). How essential that we learn to do the same.

David redirects the men's anger toward the enemy. They set out in pursuit of the Amalekites. Keep the men's weariness in mind. They still bear the trail dust of a long campaign and haven't entirely extinguished their anger at David. They don't know the Amalekites' hideout, and, if not for the sake of their loved ones, they might give up.

Indeed, two hundred do. The army reaches a brook called Besor. Soldiers wade in the creek and splash water on their faces, sink tired toes in cool mud, and stretch out on the grass. Hearing the command to move on, two hundred choose to rest. "You go on without us," they say. How tired do you have to be to abandon the hunt for your own family?

The church has its quorum of such folks. Good people. Godly people. Only hours or years ago they marched with deep resolve. But now fatigue consumes them. They're exhausted. So beat-up and worn down that they can't summon the strength to save their own flesh and blood. Old age has sucked their oxygen. Or maybe it was a deflating string of defeats. Divorce can leave you at the brook. Addiction can as well. Whatever the reason, the church has its share of people who just sit and rest.

And the church must decide. What do we do with the Brook Besor people? Berate them? Shame them? Give them a rest but measure the minutes? Or do we do what David did? *He let them stay.* David did many mighty deeds in his life. He did many foolish deeds in his life. But perhaps the noblest was this rarely discussed deed. He honored the tired soldiers.

Someday, somebody will read what David did and name their church the Congregation at Brook Besor. Isn't that what the church is intended to be? A place for soldiers to recover their strength? Brook Besor blesses rest.

Are you weary? Catch your breath. We need your strength. Are you strong? Reserve passing judgment on the tired. Odds are, at some point you'll need to plop down yourself. And when you do, Brook Besor is a good story to know. (From *Facing Your Giants* by Max Lucado.)

REACTION

7. "Plopping points" are those moments when you feel you don't have the strength to carry on. When is the last time you faced such a plopping point in your life?

8. What do you typically do when you reach your plopping point?

9. Two hundred of David's men chose to abandon the hunt for their own families at Besor. What do you think was going through these men's minds in making that decision?

10. The church has its quorum of Brook Besor people. Who are some of the "tired warriors" in your church community? What has fatigued them and sapped their strength?

11. What do you learn from David about how to treat these people?

_____

_____

_____

12. Are *you* a Brook Besor person? What do you most need to receive from God today?

_____

_____

_____

LIFE LESSONS

The final chapters in 1 Samuel are a study in contrasts. Saul, faced with the mighty Philistine army, shrinks in fear and consults a medium for guidance. David, faced with the devastation at Ziklag, rises in courage and seeks God for guidance. The Lord is with David, and he tracks down the Amalekites and recovers everything the enemy has taken. The same is not true of the one whom God has rejected as king. The Philistines close in around Saul, and his three sons—including Jonathan—are killed. Saul, sensing the end is near, instructs his armor-bearer to run him through with a sword. When the man refuses, Saul falls on his own sword. And we, the readers, are left with a cautionary tale of what happens when a person doesn't finish well. As Paul would write centuries later, "Do you not know that in a race all the runners run, but only one gets the prize? Run in such a way as to get the prize" (1 Corinthians 9:24).

DEVOTION

Father, help us to be people who seek after your own heart. Compel us to turn to you first when we are faced with all the worries and stresses of life.

Continue to guide us forward into the plans you have established for us. We pray that we will finish well and always honor you.

JOURNALING

"Two hundred of [David's men] were too exhausted to cross the valley, but David and the other four hundred continued the pursuit" (1 Samuel 30:10). You can't finish well if you are too exhausted to stay in the race. What priorities, if any, do you need to shift so that you can receive God's rest? What changes do you need to make in your schedule?

FOR FURTHER READING

To complete the book of 1 Samuel during this twelve-part study, read 1 Samuel 29:1–31:13. For more Bible passages about receiving God's rest, read Exodus 33:14; Psalm 23:1–3; Isaiah 26:3; Jeremiah 6:16; Matthew 11:28–30; John 14:27; Hebrews 4:9–11; Philippians 4:6–7.

LEADER'S GUIDE FOR SMALL GROUPS

Thank you for your willingness to lead a group through *Life Lessons from 1 Samuel*. The rewards of being a leader are different from those of participating, and we hope you find your own walk with Jesus deepened by this experience. During the twelve lessons in this study, you will guide your group through selected passages in 1 Samuel and explore the key themes of the book. There are several elements in this leader's guide that will help you as you structure your study and reflection time, so be sure to follow along and take advantage of each one.

BEFORE YOU BEGIN

Before your first meeting, make sure the group members have their own copy of the *Life Lessons from 1 Samuel* study guide so they can follow along and have their answers written out ahead of time. Alternately, you can hand out the guides at your first meeting and give the group some time to look over the material and ask any preliminary questions. Be sure to send a sheet around the room during that first meeting and have the members write down their name, phone number, and email address so you can keep in touch with them during the week.

There are several ways to structure the duration of the study. You can cover each lesson individually for a total of twelve weeks, or you can combine two lessons together per week for a total of six weeks of discussion.

You can also have the group members read just the selected passages of Scripture given in each lesson, or they can cover the entire book of 1 Samuel by reading the material listed in the "For Further Reading" section at the end of each lesson. The following table illustrates these options:

Twelve-Week Format

Week	Lessons Covered	Simplified Reading	Expanded Reading
1	Hearing God's Voice	1 Samuel 3:1–21	1 Samuel 1:1–3:21
2	A Bad Turn of Events	1 Samuel 4:1–18	1 Samuel 4:1–7:17
3	The Cry for a King	1 Samuel 8:1–22	1 Samuel 8:1–11:15
4	Obedience Is Better Than Sacrifice	1 Samuel 13:5–15; 15:10–23	1 Samuel 12:1–15:35
5	God Looks at the Heart	1 Samuel 16:1–13	1 Samuel 16:1–23
6	A Giant Problem	1 Samuel 17:1–58	1 Samuel 17:1–58
7	The Problem with Popularity	1 Samuel 18:1–16	1 Samuel 18:1–30
8	Living in Desperate Days	1 Samuel 19:4–10; 21:1–15	1 Samuel 19:1–21:15
9	Dealing with Dry Seasons	1 Samuel 23:7–29	1 Samuel 22:1–23:29
10	The God-Saturated Mind	1 Samuel 24:1–22	1 Samuel 24:1–22
11	A Well-Spoken Word	1 Samuel 25:1–35	1 Samuel 25:1–28:25
12	It's Okay to Rest	1 Samuel 30:3–25; 31:1–6	1 Samuel 29:1–31:13

Six-Week Format

Week	Lessons Covered	Simplified Reading	Expanded Reading
1	Hearing God's Voice / A Bad Turn of Events	1 Samuel 3:1–4:18	1 Samuel 1:1–7:17
2	The Cry for a King / Obedience Is Better Than Sacrifice	1 Samuel 8:1–22; 13:5–15; 15:10–23	1 Samuel 8:1–15:35
3	God Looks at the Heart / A Giant Problem	1 Samuel 16:1–13; 17:1–58	1 Samuel 16:1–17:58

Week	Lessons Covered	Simplified Reading	Expanded Reading
4	The Problem with Popularity / Living in Desperate Days	1 Samuel 18:1–16; 19:4–10; 21:1–15	1 Samuel 18:1–21:15
5	Dealing with Dry Seasons / The God-Saturated Mind	1 Samuel 23:7–24:22	1 Samuel 22:1–24:22
6	A Well-Spoken Word / It's Okay to Rest	1 Samuel 25:1–35; 30:3–25; 31:1–6	1 Samuel 25:1–31:13

Generally, the ideal size you will want for the group is between eight to ten people, which ensures everyone will have enough time to participate in discussions. If you have more people, you might want to break up the main group into smaller subgroups. Encourage those who show up at the first meeting to commit to attending the duration of the study, as this will help the group members get to know each other, create stability for the group, and help you know how to prepare each week.

Each of the lessons begins with a brief reflection that highlights the theme you will be discussing that week. As you begin your group time, have the group members briefly respond to the opening question to get them thinking about the topic at hand. Some people may want to tell a long story in response to one of these questions, but the goal is to keep the answers brief. Ideally, you want everyone in the group to get a chance to answer, so try to keep the responses to just a few minutes. If you have more talkative group members, say up front that everyone needs to limit his or her answer to two minutes.

Give the group members a chance to answer, but tell them to feel free to pass if they wish. With the rest of the study, it's generally not a good idea to have everyone answer every question—a free-flowing discussion is more desirable. But with the opening reflection question, you can go around the circle. Encourage shy people to share, but don't force them.

Before your first meeting, let the group members know how the lessons are broken down. During your group discussion time the members will be drawing on the answers they wrote for the Exploration and Reaction sections, so encourage them to always complete these ahead of time. Also, invite them to bring any questions and insights they uncovered while reading to your next meeting, especially if they had a breakthrough moment or if they didn't understand something they read.

WEEKLY PREPARATION

As the leader, there are a few things that you should do to prepare for each meeting:

- *Read through the lesson.* This will help you to become familiar with the content and know how to structure the discussion times.
- *Decide which questions you want to discuss.* Depending on how you structure your group time, you may not be able to cover every question. So select the questions ahead of time that you absolutely want the group to explore.
- *Be familiar with the questions you want to discuss.* When the group meets you'll be watching the clock, so you want to make sure you are familiar with the Bible study questions you have selected. You can then spend time in the passage again when the group meets. In this way, you'll ensure you have the passage more deeply in your mind than your group members.
- *Pray for your group.* Pray for your group members throughout the week and ask God to lead them as they study his Word.
- *Bring extra supplies to your meeting.* The members should bring their own pens for writing notes, but it's a good idea to have extras available for those who forget. You may also want to bring paper and additional Bibles.

Note that in many cases there will not be one "right" answer to the question. Answers will vary, especially when the group members are being asked to share their personal experiences.

STRUCTURING THE DISCUSSION TIME

You will need to determine with your group how long you want to meet each week so you can plan your time accordingly. Generally, most groups like to meet for either sixty minutes or ninety minutes, so you could use one of the following schedules:

Section	60 Minutes	90 Minutes
WELCOME (members arrive and get settled)	5 minutes	10 minutes
REFLECTION (discuss the opening question for the lesson)	10 minutes	15 minutes
DISCUSSION (discuss the Bible study questions in the Exploration and Reaction sections)	35 minutes	50 minutes
PRAYER/CLOSING (pray together as a group and dismiss)	10 minutes	15 minutes

As the group leader, it is up to you to keep track of the time and keep things moving along according to your schedule. You might want to set a timer for each segment so both you and the group members know when your time is up. (Note that there are some good phone apps for timers that play a gentle chime or other pleasant sound instead of a disruptive noise.) Don't feel pressured to cover every question you have selected if the group has a good discussion going. Again, it's not necessary to go around the circle and make everyone share.

Don't be concerned if the group members are silent or slow to share. People are often quiet when they are pulling together their ideas, and this might be a new experience for them. Just ask a question and let it hang in the air until someone shares. You can then say, "Thank you. What about others? What came to you when you reflected on the passage?"

GROUP DYNAMICS

Leading a group through *Life Lessons from 1 Samuel* will prove to be highly rewarding both to you and your group members—but that doesn't mean you will not encounter any challenges along the way! Discussions can get off track. Group members may not be sensitive to the needs and ideas of others. Some might worry they will be expected to talk about matters that make them feel awkward. Others may express comments that result in disagreements. To help ease this strain on you and the group, consider the following ground rules:

- When someone raises a question or comment that is off the main topic, suggest you deal with it another time, or, if you feel led to go in that direction, let the group know you will be spending some time discussing it.
- If someone asks a question you don't know how to answer, admit it and move on. At your discretion, invite group members to comment on questions that call for personal experience.
- If you find one or two people are dominating the discussion time, direct a few questions to others in the group. Outside the main group time, ask the more dominating members to help you draw out the quieter ones. Work to make them a part of the solution instead of the problem.
- When a disagreement occurs, encourage the group members to process the matter in love. Encourage those on opposite sides to restate what they heard the other side say about the matter, and then invite each side to evaluate if that perception is accurate. Lead the group in examining other Scriptures related to the topic and look for common ground.

When any of these issues arise, encourage your members to follow the words: "Love one another" (John 13:34), "If it is possible, as far as it depends on you, live at peace with everyone" (Romans 12:18), and, "Be quick to listen, slow to speak and slow to become angry" (James 1:19).

Thank you again for taking the time to lead your group. May God reward your efforts and dedication and make your time together in this study fruitful for his kingdom.